The Buffalo Spirit

A Memoir of the Road Less Traveled By

Dale Healey

Lexingford Publishing LLC
New York Ottawa San Francisco Hong Kong
www.lexingfordpublishingllc.com

ISBN 13: 978-0996394895
ISBN-10: 0996394893

Photographic and Design Assistance: LaPointe Illustrations www.catherinelapointe.com

Cover Art Photograph: Denise Schryver. Used with permission. Author Photo: Jennifer N. Easton. Used with permission.

Set in Garamond 12 point.
First Edition
Printed and Published in the United States
Deposited in the Library of Congress

Lexingford Publishing LLC
New York Ottawa San Francisco Hong Kong
www.lexingfordpublishingllc.com

For those who hear an inner voice, and go seeking out its source.

Preface

The following is a true account of my experiences with Native American medicine men and how, through their influences, I was called to raise buffalo for the past twenty-two years. Or perhaps they raised me, given the extraordinary events which shaped my journey.

Dale Healey
Potsdam, New York
September, 2016

Dedication

This work is dedicated to the Native American spiritual leaders who generously shared their time, wisdom, and ceremonies with me. I recognize with profound gratitude that few "outsiders" are given access to the cultural and spiritual worlds they opened for me.

I also dedicate this book to my parents, who were early examples of kindness, love, and integrity in my life.

Finally, I remember with great fondness Thomas Asmondy ("Ol' Eyes On Fire"). I speak for those of us you called "brother" when I say "you live within our hearts."

Acknowledgments

My thanks to those who have nudged this project on its way. Helen Marie Johnson-Kenny, I'll always remember and cherish your initial encouragement over a beer to turn a lifetime of memories into a book that might interest and influence others. David Sommerstein, of North Country Public Radio, your interview about my raising of bison ended with a provocative question—a catalyst, really—that led me to take seriously the task and joy of telling this story. Brook Lynch of the St. Lawrence County Arts Council, thank you for your encouragement after reading my first few chapters and your valuable suggestions. Jennifer N. Easton, for a lifetime of friendship and for your commitment to improve the lives of others through the programs you have initiated and supported. Gaia Reblitz, a wise woman, loyal friend, and teacher.

Mary Ellen, my dear wife, you have been by my side throughout the ups and downs of completing this project. For your patience and support, I express my love and deep thanks. And finally, to Art Bell and his staff at Lexingford Publishing LLC, for guidance in seeing a manuscript through the process of becoming the book I envisioned.

Table of Contents

Introduction

When we reflect on our lives, we sometimes discover a common thread winding through seemingly random events which shaped our future. As I look back over the years, I realize my life has been shaped by the completely unexplained and unexpected vision I had, at the age of thirteen, of an old Indian man in the woods near my home. Now, more than fifty-five years after that vision in the woods, and over thirty-five years since I first encountered Native American medicine men, I feel my teachers are calling on me to share my story, and through it to share a glimpse of their wisdom.

This memoir is about my time with amazing individuals who exposed me directly to the Spirit World and, as a consequence, brought forth my connection with the flesh and spirit of buffalo. My hope is that the reader will find something in my story that will speak to some aspect of their own inner or external life, or even their curiosity about fleeting and mysterious moments seemingly filled with feeling and meaning.

For nearly fourteen years, beginning in 1978, when I was thirty-one, I traveled the back roads of the West, much of the time by myself. My travels took me from the Colorado Rockies to the Pacific Coast, and from Canada to southern Mexico. I sought the solitude of quiet, lonesome places, off the beaten path, where few people ventured. Since I did not have a career to tie me down or a family to support, my lifestyle allowed me the freedom to go where and when I chose. The lack of responsibilities to others allowed me to be open to whatever circumstances might arise. I thrived on the uncertainty of what would happen next. I held a belief that life is "magical" and that something would guide me to where I should be, and what

I would do. I never had much money, but always found enough work to keep me in food and gas. Never motivated by financial success or social status, I pursued a life of freedom lived close to nature. As I followed my heart, each situation would unfold and lead me to the next interesting experience. What had begun as simply a search for a new job in a different environment evolved into a psychological and spiritual journey.

An inner longing, perhaps initiated by that early vision of an old Indian man when I was thirteen, caused me to seek out Native American spiritual leaders. I was fortunate to be invited into their homes and participate in their ceremonies. The people and places I encountered were truly more amazing than what I could have ever imagined. Pushing back my natural tendency toward shyness, I managed to summon the courage to step into unknown places and circumstances, some incredibly rewarding, others very challenging and often confusing, especially, I must admit, where some women were concerned.

Sometimes I had comfortable cabins to live in. More often I stayed in old sheds, lean-to's, or teepees without running water or other amenities. There were times when I simply lived out of my Jeep or tent. Sometimes months went by without a visit to a town or a store. The only people I was in contact with were the few others who lived at those remote locations. My social life and female companionship varied greatly depending upon where I was living at the time. Sometimes my social contacts were fulfilling and memorable. Many other times these connections with others reinforced my deep sense of loneliness.

But when I was with the Native elders I felt like I was absorbing their ways and instructions into my being. A deep sense of meaning and wonder countered any feelings of loneliness I might have felt. With each new vista of experience, I imagined my father looking through my eyes so he could share in my wanderings. I felt at times that I was living not only for myself but for others that I carried within, literally in genetic terms and figuratively in my heritage. With that thought foremost in mind, I conclude this Introduction with special memories of my father:

Dad,
Somehow I feel you are with me in my wanderings,
Somehow you see the mountains through my eyes,
Somehow you feel the earth beneath my feet,
Somehow you hear the wind blowing around me.

When I look out over the desert,
When I look out from a mountain top,
When I look out upon the sea,
When I look up at the stars above,
When I am alone in nature,
You are there with me.

In an effort at full transparency, I must reveal that several names have been changed to honor the requests and protect the privacy of some of my indigenous friends. Similarly, I have not revealed the exact locations where their spiritual rites or daily lives are lived out to this day. I have quoted individuals carefully through notes I took at the time or when particularly potent words or phrases they used were imprinted in my mind. Grandfather Semu Huaute allowed me to tape-record his conversations and teaching while he was residing at Odin Falls Ranch.

I do not pretend to speak for Native people or to be an "expert" about their complex and millennia-old cultures. My narrative is simply a plain-language sharing of my experiences as a relatively naïve and uninformed country boy—but one whose life was influenced and changed forever by my time spent with very special Native elders. Because their wisdom may never reach a wider audience through other channels, I hope that in some respects my story gives a glimpse of their profound story as well.

Be aware that this book includes descriptions of ceremonies involving the ingestion of psycho-active mushrooms, peyote and datura. I want to caution anyone from using these powerful plants for recreational purposes. They are not something to take lightly or to be used without the guidance of a knowledgeable, experienced and trusted guide. Without proper preparation for such experiences, including a settled, receptive state of mind, the ingestion of these substances can be damaging to one's body and spirit. Datura is especially dangerous and potentially deadly in the hands of those not thoroughly knowledgeable in its preparation and use.

Chapter One

A New Life in the Rockies

It was a typical cold, gray day in northern New York when Charlie arrived to pick me up that afternoon in early January, 1978. We'd both attended a Christmas party hosted by a mutual friend ten days earlier. There Charlie told me he was going out west to look for work. His plan was to visit friends for a couple days near Vail, Colorado, then head for the warmth of Texas to get a construction job for the winter.

"Did you hear the one about two salesmen traveling through the West"? Charlie asked, as I put my duffle bag in the trunk of his Chevy sedan. He was an easy-going guy with the gift of gab and seemed to have a joke for any situation. I don't remember the punchline to his joke. Perhaps we two were the punchline as we set out high on hope and low on money for our great Western adventure.

The Rockies represented new possibilities and a fresh start. I was ready for a new beginning. My wife and I had separated a few months earlier. I was seeking employment for the winter not only to keep body and soul together but also to keep my mind from drifting back to old arguments and regrets. I decided to go west with Charlie and work construction somewhere until spring, and then return home for my summer job with the Department of Environmental Conservation. At that moment of decision, I had no idea I would spend the next fourteen years in the West, nor did it occur to me that riding West with Charlie (himself of Iroquois heritage) would be the beginning of my life-changing engagement with Native people.

Taking four hour shifts at the wheel, one of us could doze while the other drove. While Charlie slept, I reminisced about my life over the past few years to lay the ground-work in my mind for whatever might unfold next. I hoped that pieces from the past would come together, like a puzzle, into a sudden whole.

Three years before I'd been employed with a large insurance company in Rochester, N. Y. I couldn't see anything of the world outside. My view was only of rows of desks, fluorescent lights, telephones, computers and file cabinets. I somehow managed to avoid the endless series of company golf leagues, bowling teams and weekend retreats. Everything revolved around the company. "So this is the life of a working stiff," I mumbled to myself more than once. It all felt somehow unreal to me—a gossamer world that could be brushed away with one swipe of the hand.

At one point I was told by an upper level manager that he couldn't understand why I'd been selected for management training. He was frank: "You don't fit the mold. You're supposed to be married and have at least two kids so the company can control you easier. They like to have you so strapped with family expenses and a mortgage that you'll be desperate enough to put up with the pressure and work your butt off for the company for forty years or so."

I saw the life force draining out of many of my fellow employees. They seemed to be trading in their personal truths to climb the promotional ladder within the all-important company. In a way I saw them as victims, caught up in the cruel game of always needing to earn more money as proof that they were worthy of promotion. When storms came rolling through their lives—divorce, ill health, problems with their kids—they never quite saw the connection between their personal losses and what they were giving of themselves to the company. "Getting ahead" seemed to be their robotic response to life's hard times.

I don't think I was wiser than the men and women I worked with. I credit the country boy in me for the growing sense of spiritual suffocation as my business tie cinched tighter and tighter around my neck. I vividly recall precious moments while sitting at my desk but in truth off on a daydream about being in the fields and woods surrounding my boyhood home. I realized the manager who told me I didn't fit the mold was correct. Already in my mid- twenties I knew that I wanted—I needed--more from life than office walls, my files, and my stapler. To his amazement (no one quit the company), I gave my one-sentence resignation letter to my department head, cut off my tie, and dropped it in the waste basket.

Of course I took the expected flak from my parents and others who thought I was crazy to quit a "good" job and give up the security of a regular pay check. What exactly were my plans, they asked. Did I think I had a future as a drop-out (their polite word for "bum")? It did little good to explain to them that I had no interest in spending my life in a dreary office attempting to live someone else's life. True, I had given up financial security—but I had rescued my life.

After resigning, I took my tent, canoe and camping supplies and drove to Cranberry Lake in the Adirondack Mountains of New York State. I paddled the canoe six miles to the wilderness side of the lake and set up camp on a high peninsula. It was a short paddle from my tent site to the rustic Wild Cliff Lodge, which is only accessible by boat at the far end of the lake from the hamlet of Cranberry Lake. I spent most of that summer hiking the trails and fishing the wilderness ponds which surround the lake. To be truthful, I didn't feel heroic or vindicated. Often I felt bored or cold or bug-bitten or all three. But I was no longer wearing the noose.

As summer came to an end I felt the urge to travel to the Southwest. With part of my final payment of company stock, I bought a pick-up truck with a camper shell. Together with my younger brother Bob and another friend, I left New York State in late fall with what felt like a bulging wallet containing the eight hundred dollars remaining from my savings.

We made time quickly across the Northeast and Plains states. Within a few days, energized by the pulse of youth, we found ourselves exploring little outposts and small villages in New Mexico and Arizona—the more obscure the better, as far as we were concerned. We wanted to discover something—Lord knows what—either in the dust of the little towns or within ourselves. Our longest sojourn in one place was a week in Tombstone, drinking with the locals and trying to avoid the tourist clap-trap. From there we drove the short distance to Nogales, Arizona, where we caught a train to Mazatlan, Mexico. I don't recall if I had read Jack Kerouac's "On the Road" novel—but we were definitely "living the life" of young men ferocious about their freedom and seemingly endless options.

After spending five months in the Southwest we returned home in the spring of 1974. I got a job with the Department of Environmental Conservation clearing hiking and snowmobile trails in the Adirondack Mountains from Wanakena to Long Lake.

Early that summer I met Michele, a student nurse from my home town. Our relationship developed quickly and we began living together that fall. Since she was a student and my income was quite limited, we couldn't afford comfortable housing. We spent the winter—the Adirondack winter, to be brutally clear--in an old, cold single-wide mobile home. But our thoughts were warmed that winter by our constant chatter about a plan to build a log cabin on a thirty acre forested parcel of land that I co-owned with my father.

Spring couldn't arrive fast enough for us to begin. Even with frost still on the ground I started cutting hemlock trees to construct the cabin. Using an old tractor, we skidded the logs to a clearing in the center of the land. There we peeled the bark from the logs and felt the heady combination of young love and a pioneering spirit. We were married in July and spent the summer finishing the cabin with some help from my brother, Bob, and Michele's brother, Les, and sister, Linda. We completed covering the roof the first week of November. King and queen in their self-made palace, we spent our first night in the cabin sleeping on the floor. We awoke to reality: winter had set in and more than a foot of snow had fallen during the night.

Our "mansion" (in our minds) was connected to what there was of civilization by a narrow, winding road I'd cut through the trees. Even in good weather, negotiating this goat-path to reach the top of the hill and the main road by car was a challenge. Dick Benson, an old farmer friend I had known since childhood, told me, "You have to set your jaw just right to drive up that hill." His advice about setting my jaw seemed to work until snow continued to fall for several days, building up to the point we were not able to plow our way up the steep, winding road up to the highway. This meant we had to walk the quarter mile from the cabin up a hill through deep snow to reach our vehicle, which we kept near the highway during the winter months. But even in heavy snow we cherished our hideaway. Several acres near the center of the property were covered with large hemlocks. A small stream ran through the length of our land (and in fact does so today).

We had enclosed a twenty-four by thirty-two-foot structure, but lacked funds to improve it further. The cabin was warm and dry, but had no electricity, running water or telephone service. We carried water from a nearby creek for cooking and sponge baths, and Michele prepared meals on an antique wood cook stove. In the evenings she studied by light from a kerosene lamp. Our "bathroom" was an outhouse, the subject of more scowls than humor. On a particularly dark night, Michele found herself sitting in the outhouse accompanied, to her immediate revulsion, by a three-foot grass snake. She howled for help and I howled with laughter—not my wisest moment as a supportive companion.

"Mom asked if we're going to have a central vacuum system," Michele queried one day. That question highlighted the disconnect in our two visions of married life. The log cabin, the winding road, the outhouse, and all the rest had been largely my vision. They were not Michele's. As our living conditions became more and more challenging for Michele, I realized that she had grown up accustomed to having every modern convenience. Nor did it help that we had hardly any money for necessities, much less for fun or for her tuition as a nursing student. A little more than two years after staking out our log cabin in the woods our marriage began to unravel. It became obvious to us both that we were going in separate directions and wanted very different things. When she moved to the nearby village in the fall of 1977 I felt the emptiness of the cabin. The gray winter days were wearing on me and the nights were long and lonesome. I was marking time, it seemed, and felt that I was sinking a bit lower each day in my spirits.

Fast-forward again to Christmas, 1977, and Charlie's tempting invitation to "come on and go West with me." My marriage over and the walls of my cabins closing in, I knew I needed to join him.

We were about seventy miles east of Denver when Charlie yelled, "Check it out! There's the Rockies." I opened my eyes to see the first rays of the morning sun reflecting off the snowcapped peaks west of the city. The inspiring view, along with our anticipation and excitement, was cause for celebration. "To the Rockies," I offered, as I cracked open a fifth of Jack Daniels and passed it to Charlie. Although It was early in the day, it seemed appropriate to celebrate the view and the adventures that awaited us.

A construction boom was underway in Vail at the time. The day after we arrived we both found jobs helping to build a large ski chalet. We stayed with Charlie's friends for a week until we located a rental house in Minturn, a few miles west of Vail.

Due to all the construction jobs it was quickly obvious that there were more far more men than women in the area. Single guys like me focused our hopes on meeting women at places like the laundromat or grocery store without much success. Spending time in the taverns was expensive and crawling with tourists. Many of the locals avoided the bar scene not only because of the out-of-town clientele but also because we wanted to meet locals from the area. I had a couple of casual relationships during the spring and early summer, but nothing meaningful. Charlie, adept at smooth talking, found a new girlfriend shortly after our arrival and they eventually relocated to Sun Valley, Idaho.

My days off were often spent cross-country skiing and snow shoeing in the mountains surrounding Vail with other single guys who were avid back country skiers. Days off work in the summer allowed time for river rafting, hiking and exploring the Rockies. I worked in Vail from early January through June, but began to feel a restlessness and loneliness that had become familiar by now. I felt confined in the narrow valley.

So six months after arriving in Colorado I drove north to Steamboat Springs. The "feel" was different here, with many horse and cattle ranches in the area. Having grown up on a horse farm the western flavor and open terrain of the area appealed to me. I had no trouble finding a job, but housing was another matter. The developers in the area were focused on building expensive condominiums and duplexes, but there was very little affordable housing for working people. Newcomers crammed into apartments and less expensive rental units. Sometimes even large closets (originally intended for the wardrobes of the rich) were used as sleeping areas. I recognized in my search for housing that I was changing. While I needed to find cheap housing, I wanted my privacy and wasn't interested in moving in with strangers. My earnings were limited, so the less I needed to put out for housing, the more I'd have left for road trips and other adventures. Since my days and evenings were filled with activity, I simply needed a place to sleep and store my few belongings.

Exploring the area, I spotted an old cabin tucked away among the trees on a ranch at the base of Rabbit Ears Pass. I inquired about the vacant cabin, which wasn't advertised because most people wouldn't have considered it habitable. It had no insulation or running water, and had only been used as a summer bunk house for ranch hands in years past. The owners agreed to rent it to me for one hundred dollars per month, which turned out to be more than it was worth. Shortly after moving into the cabin that fall, the carburetor in my vehicle malfunctioned and it took a while to get the correct parts. Lacking "wheels" with winter setting in, I hadn't had a chance to put up much fire wood or make improvements to the cabin. There wasn't much reason to stay home.

Looking for some social interaction, I went to a local tavern one evening after work. The bar at "Dos Amigos" was already crowded when I arrived. Finding a spot to squeeze in at the bar, I ordered a draft beer. As I turned from the bar I was face to face with a tall, attractive young woman, with long dark hair and a nice smile. "Hi," she said. She told me she had recently moved here from southern California. A couple of drinks later, more conversation revealed she was twenty-four, and was from a well-to-do, but broken family. Although we were from very different backgrounds and economic circumstances, I immediately felt an easy-going compatibility with Susan. The conversation that followed and her comfortable manner gave me the feeling she'd known me for years, although we were complete strangers. After a few beers I decided it was time for me to make the three mile walk back to my cabin since I had to be up early for work the next day. "Oh, Dale," she said with concern, "you can't walk home in this weather! Why don't you spend the night at my apartment and go to work from there tomorrow." I was physically attracted to Susan, but even more taken with her warm, caring attitude. That evening was the beginning of a relaxed, sporadic relationship that continued until I left Steamboat nearly three years later.

Initially our evenings together were spent at her upscale apartment in the village. Curious about my lifestyle and eager to see my cabin, Susan accompanied me home one cold December night. Her background had never exposed her to such rough living circumstances and she was in complete disbelief to discover that I lived without running water or other conveniences. Thanks to her good-natured attitude we made the best of an otherwise awkward situation. She wasted no time in encouraging me to find better living accommodations for the remaining winter months.

There was a little pond near the cabin which I would cross on the ice to get buckets of water from the spillway at the far end. On a relatively warm day in January,1979, I took my axe and a bucket and started across the pond to get water. When I reached the center of the pond the ice suddenly gave way beneath me, and I plunged through into the icy water. As I popped up sputtering from the frigid water, my first thought was, "Oh shit, I'm all alone out here and there's nobody around to help me." Fortunately, I'd held onto the axe and was able to take a swing and drive the axe head into more solid ice. Gradually, I inched my way up the axe handle pulling my upper body onto firmer ice. My chest now out of the water, I cautiously wiggled the axe head from its grip in the ice and swung it into the ice again, slightly further from the hole I was in. Repeating this procedure a couple more times I eventually reached thicker ice where I could spread out and crawl to the edge of the pond. Soaked and shivering, I laughed at the absurdity of my situation as I trudged back to the cold cabin without my bucket of water. "Jesus, man," I muttered to myself. "This is 1979, not 1779. What were you thinking?" I was alone, with no fire wood, and no fresh water, but I had survived and I felt grateful to be alive. I didn't know enough about hypothermia to be truly afraid.

A few weeks later, on a frigid February night I crawled into my sleeping bag, bundled under every blanket I had. I slept soundly, thanks to the amount of alcohol I consumed the night before. But I awoke in the early morning amazed to find that the cabin door had blown open during the night. A three foot-high, eight foot-long snow drift reached to the foot of my bed. Lying in bed, I looked through the open door to see the brilliant morning sun reflected off the snow on the east wall of the cliffs of the Flattop Mountains across the valley. When I crawled out from my sleeping bag and turned the radio on, I learned that it was thirty-eight degrees below zero. The view of the cliffs reflecting the morning sun was breathtaking, but not worth freezing to death. As beautiful as that scene was I finally decided it was time to take Susan's advice and find a more comfortable—and safe--living space.

After helping construct a log house for a couple of

months, I found employment with the Steamboat Ski Corporation so I could take advantage of the recreational opportunities and free ski pass. For the next three years I worked for the Corporation as a carpenter on the maintenance crew.

One sunny March afternoon, I drove to the top of Rabbit Ears Pass, elevation 9000+ feet, to go cross-country skiing by myself. The sky was clear and the temperature was mild. I dressed light, wearing just a windbreaker over my sweater, and carrying a fanny pack containing water, chocolate, trail mix, a lighter, and candle. Skiing due north, moving along quickly, and inspired by the beauty of the day and the surroundings, I gave no thought to the absence of other skiers. There were a couple other cars in the parking lot when I arrived, but those folks must have taken the shorter loops closer to the parking area.

Stopping for a moment to look around and take in the view, I noticed a very dark, foreboding sky to the south. Unnoticed, it had moved in behind me. Immediately I turned around and started skiing back towards the trailhead where I'd left my Jeep.

A moment later I was in a whiteout. The snow was falling so fast that it had covered my original tracks. As the wind picked up, the heavy snow was blowing directly at me, continually covering my goggles. I was caught in a blizzard. The visibility was so poor I could see only a few feet ahead of me. I was exerting so much energy skiing through deep snow that I wasn't aware of the temperature dropping. Although I had a good sense of direction, the blinding snow caused me to veer off the trail, gradually dropping too far in elevation to return to the trailhead. Now it was getting dark. I was exhausted and hungry from pushing through the deep, heavy snow. The steep climb to the summit of the pass, back to my vehicle, seemed impossible. Still confident about my general sense of direction, I thought if I kept heading south into the storm, at some point I'd come out to the road leading to the base of the pass. When I got into thick timber with lots of blow downs and snags I became nervous and tired to the core. Darkness had fully set in. I forced myself to stop to rest and eat some chocolate and granola. I shook my head and tried to gather my senses. With a bit of alarm I felt the dampness from my sweat turning cold on my skin. I realized I had to get moving again before hypothermia set in. In the darkness I picked my way through the dense forest, crawling under limbs and climbing over dead logs. At times I removed my skis and carried them because it was otherwise impossible to get through the snags and thick timber.

Eventually I reached a rock cliff which dropped fifteen to twenty feet into the shadowy darkness below. I wondered if I went down the cliff if I would get trapped by higher cliffs further on. I decided under the circumstances I didn't have enough reserve strength to back track, so I threw my skis and poles over the cliff and jumped. The snow was deep enough to cushion my landing, and after I dug myself out of the snow I pushed on. I considered abandoning my skis to make it easier to climb the steep slope opposite the cliff, but resisted that urge, knowing I might need them further on. After struggling my way through deep snow and rough terrain a while longer I eventually came down another steep embankment. To my immense relief, I realized I had reached the road. Knowing that I couldn't make the climb back up to the parking area where I had left my Jeep, my only option at that point was to put my skis on and make the several mile trek to the village. Although I was soaked with sweat and completely exhausted I knew it was a matter of forcing myself to push on, shoving one foot in front of the other. When I finally arrived home I collapsed into a deep, dreamless sleep. I didn't think about how close I had come to death in the blizzard.

Two days later, after the snowplows were able to clear the road to the trail head, I retrieved my Jeep. I realized it was a combination of my ignorance about mountain weather and desire to be alone in nature that could have cost me my life. It sunk in that the natural beauty I so loved could also become a natural disaster.

During the summers our crew at the ski area worked ten hour days Monday through Thursday, so we had three days off every weekend. During the weekends of my first two summers there, I worked for a local rancher/outfitter who kept twenty horses and a mule on a four-hundred-acre ranch surrounded by national forest, about fifteen miles north of town.

I'd grown up on a horse farm in northern New York. Horses had been a major part of my life from age seven through my high school years. We had thirty head of horses which my three brothers, my sister Janis and I trained and exhibited at local fairs and horse shows throughout the summer. We also had a few head of beef cattle, a dozen chickens, and a large, productive garden. When I was ten I started a little business giving pony rides, and three years later began teaching horsemanship to Girl Scout troops and individuals. Every Sunday during the summer my brothers, my sister and I would attend local fairs and horse shows. Janis rode English in pleasure and three-gated classes, but we boys all rode Western in the quarter- and half-mile races and "rough-rider" contests. My younger brothers, Dick and Bob, also competed in team roping events.

My brother Dave, a talented athlete, was involved in team sports throughout the year. On the other hand, my aptitude and interest for sports was limited. But I could handle a horse.

When I was thirteen I raced my mare in the

youths' quarter- mile race at the county fair and came in second behind a very fast stallion. As soon as that race ended, my brother Dave, three years older than I, informed me that I would be riding his horse, Sunsan, in the adult half-mile race. Sunsan, a relatively small horse, had shorter legs than most other horses in the competition. But he was very fast and had a lot of heart. He couldn't stand to have another horse ahead of him. Dave had trained Sunsan as a colt and had always placed either first or second. He warned me, "You'd better come in at least in second place or I'll kick your ass!"

Sunsan always knew when he was going to race and became extremely excited, requiring both my brother and my dad to attempt to keep him from lunging away as I mounted him.

It took all my strength to hold Sunsan back as he bounded toward the starting gate. He was continually lunging forward and my young arms were aching from holding him from breaking into a full gallop before the gun went off. We had drawn the outside position, number thirteen, while our toughest competition, a tall quarter horse mare, had the number one position next to the rail. Her rider was an older, very experienced horseman named Rolly. Just as I got Sunsan up to the starting line, the gun went off. I gave him a free rein and he bolted out in front of most of the pack and cut in behind the number one horse, hugging the inside rail. When Rolly's horse moved slightly away from the rail on the back-stretch, Sunsan took advantage of the opening and started gaining on the mare.

Just as we were nearly neck and neck, Rolly used his long reins to slap my mount in the face several times before I was able to pull Sunsan back slightly to protect him. When we got to the back turn the mare moved away from the rail a little more and we were running neck to neck. But as we closed in on the finish line, the mare's long legs gave her the advantage and she pulled past us to win. At least we came in second place and I was spared an ass kicking from my big brother. Sunsan's record was left untarnished and he became somewhat of a legend in the north country for his accumulated wins over many years of gaming and racing.

* * * *

My weekend job at the ranch in Colorado was to wrangle the horses down from the foothills each weekend and take guests out on trail rides into the mountains to view deer and elk. I kept a tall, long-legged gelding near the cabin to locate the other horses and chase them back to the corral where I would saddle them for the tourists. The big gelding could cover a lot of ground fast with his long stride, which helped me to locate the other horses on the four hundred acres relatively quickly.

There were also cattle grazing in the mountain meadows. On two occasions while I was leading groups up the narrow trails through densely wooded sections, we encountered angry bulls blocking the trail. The bulls would snort and paw the ground, indicating they were ready to charge at us. This section of trail was steep and narrow, so there was no way to either turn back or get past the bulls. I would call their "bluffs" by swinging my rope and yelling, while charging my horse directly at them. Not certain my charge would scare the bulls, it seemed to be the only way to prevent the bulls from charging into the horses and riders in my care. Fortunately, at the last second before we collided, the bulls turned and ran back to their herds, allowing the group to continue up the steep trail.

Late in the summer my employer and I hauled the horses and mule on a trailer ten miles further up into the mountains, where he had a base camp with a large cabin and corrals. He would take groups of five people to the base camp for five-day outings to photograph elk. They'd spend their days taking photos in the wilderness, returning to the base camp each evening.

I was quite surprised to look out from my cabin at the ranch one morning to see the old mule leading all the horses back to the corral. They must have escaped the corral at the base camp and decided life at the ranch was easier. Fortunately, they were all together and none had injuries. The old mule was definitely their trusted leader, and I was relieved that she brought them all safely home.

* * * *

One of my responsibilities at the ski area during the winter months was to do occasional shifts as a night security person at the gondola station midway up the mountain. Just before dark I would take a radio phone and drive a snowmobile up to the gondola station for the night. Being alone up there at night was both eerie and somewhat mystical. I'd ride the snowmobile to an open area where I could see the lights of the village below. The village looked so warm, cozy and silent from this perspective. Everything was covered in a soft blanket of snow and the lights from the village told of people snuggled inside enjoying tasty food, drink, and musical entertainment.

I felt like the lone wolf looking down on the lights of the settlers' cabins below on a lonesome winter night. I was the misfit, the outcast, peering down on civilization, aware of it, but not feeling a part of it. How strange it felt, especially compared to the daytime when there were hundreds of skiers on the mountain and all kinds of activity. Eventually I came to realize that I wasn't really part of this culture. I was more truly myself as the lone wolf on the mountain than as one of the crowd in the village. I was more comfortable with the trees and the elements than in social settings. My connection to work and society felt like temporary necessities—stopgaps to provide me with the time and financial freedom to escape by myself to the natural world.

As a resort town, Steamboat had many restaurants and saloons where young single people worked and partied. There were often kegs of beer in our locker room at the end of the day with several bars holding happy hours just a short walk from the building. The rational of "attitude adjustment," meant using alcohol to deal with the frustrations incurred from constantly dealing with tourists. It was difficult to resist the partying, and I participated willingly. Although it had all been part of my lifestyle since my teenage years, it was beginning to hold less interest for me now. I enjoyed the camaraderie of many people there, but perhaps because I was a few years older than most of my co-workers, my priorities were different. I enjoyed skiing, but saw it as a temporary diversion. It certainly wasn't my life focus, as it was for many there. Once again, I felt it was time for some kind of change.

Chapter Two

The Angel and The Outlaws

It was April 1981 and the ski season had just ended. The melting snow had turned the earth to mud and I longed for dry ground, dry air and sunshine. Each spring for the past two years I'd headed for the Southwest to soak up the sun and the quietness of the land. A year earlier I had been drawn to places such as Oraibi, Indian Wells, and Second Mesa, ancient Hopi and Navaho [Dinah] villages, where there seemed to be little more than what was required for a basic existence.

Some of the homes--small, nearly windowless stone structures--probably predated the arrival of Columbus in the Americas. No running water or electricity served these villages. Old men using crude hoes somehow manage to urge corn sprouts from the dry, sandy soil, perhaps more through their prayers and intention instead of any help from the environment. Yet life in these villages, existing somehow beyond the measure of time, was more directly connected to a purposeful existence and seemed more meaningful to me than the relatively affluent, fun-focused lifestyle at the ski areas. The passage of time here did not seem relevant in the same way as I'd found it to be elsewhere.

This particular Spring I wanted to spend some time by myself in Monument Valley in the four corners area of Arizona, Utah, Colorado, and New Mexico. I had been intrigued with the inspiring rock formations there ever since I had first visited the area in 1973 on my way back from Mexico. Six years later I had camped there briefly with some friends after a week of hiking and camping in the Grand Canyon. Now I felt called back there to immerse myself in the quiet desert, where time seemed to stand still and only the shadows moved with the passing of the day.

I packed my camping gear and old shotgun in my Jeep Wagoner and drove west into Utah, taking the less traveled roads south. Traveling alone, camping in remote areas, I found that the shotgun gave me a sense of security. It had come in handy a year earlier when I used it to discourage a couple of guys who were attempting to steal my vehicle at a camping area north of Sedona, Arizona.

I decided to visit Zion National Park in the southwest corner of Utah on my way to Monument Valley. It was getting dark by the time I arrived. I drove into a narrow canyon where I decided to spend the night, but once I'd settled into my sleeping bag I had a certain foreboding feeling that something about this place didn't seem right. Getting spooked, I quickly left the area to find another place to camp. The following morning I returned out of curiosity to see if I could get some understanding of why I'd had such a strong negative feeling about the place. Walking the trail at the end of the road I saw a sign which said something to this effect: "Local tribes would visit this area during daylight but would always leave before darkness." I never found out why the place was to be avoided at night, but apparently my intuition was functioning properly. It was, however, a beautiful setting with nothing disturbing in the daylight. But with darkness came mystery.

Spending the next two days hiking in Zion, I hiked the steep wall of Angels' Landing before traveling south into Arizona. I was not comfortable around steep drop-offs, and the final leg of the trail was very challenging for me. Hand grips along the wall helped prevent one from slipping and falling more than two thousand feet to the valley floor. But due to my fear of heights, the climb really tested my nerves. I knew I had to work through my anxiety before I could tolerate returning to the cliff for the descent. While taking in the view from the peak in a strong wind, I managed to quiet myself by lying belly-down against the hard stone of the summit, letting my fears be absorbed by the rock beneath me. However, descending was even more of a challenge for me than the climb had been, perhaps because I was looking down and more aware of the sheer drop. I did make it down safely, but my nerves were frazzled. The following morning I headed southeast towards Monument Valley.

As I crossed into Arizona my vehicle was low on fuel and I was thirsty for something other than stale canteen water. At Tuba City, a small junction east of the Grand Canyon, I filled the Jeep up with gas and bought a Dr. Pepper to quench my thirst. Heading east into the desert I popped open the soda, took a swig, and noticed an old Native man hitchhiking. When he got into my vehicle, I handed him the can of soda, thinking he was thirsty from standing in the sun. Still thirsty myself, I thought he might take a sip and hand it back. Instead the old man immediately chugged all the soda down and flung the can out the window.

"Were you thirsty"? I asked jokingly, but soon realized he didn't understand me. A few moments later I began to hear what I initially thought was crying coming from the old man, but then it became apparent that he was singing in his language. Maybe this was his way of showing appreciation for the ride. Anyway, the situation struck me as humorous. Here I was with this old Navajo man and we couldn't communicate. I don't know how far he needs to go, or where he wants to get out, and I can't imagine what's going to happen next.

After I had been driving about half hour the old man seemed to have fallen asleep; I'm concerned I'll drive past where he wants to get out. I started singing "You Can't Roller Skate Through A Buffalo Herd," singing louder and louder until he woke up. A little while later he pointed to the left and I spotted a Jeep trail on the north side of the road. When I pulled over to let him out, he reached over, grasped my hand in both of his hands, and spoke for a couple of moments in his language. It seemed he was praying, but I had no rational way to know that. With a semi-toothless grin he got out of the Jeep in the middle of nowhere, walked up the trail and disappeared in the desert brush.

That old Navajo man stirred up the memory of an experience I'd had as a boy in the woods near my home.

* * * *

In April of 1959, when I was thirteen I was eager to go into the woods with the bow and arrows my parents had given me for Christmas. As I started across the field heading for the woods along the river I nearly stepped on a grass snake. I stood back in amazement. The little snake was coiled up on itself in a perfect circle about six inches in diameter and four inches high, like a perfectly coiled rope. I'd never seen a snake in that position before and it struck me as something special and unique. After a moment or two of awe, I said so long, leaving the creature as it was, and continued toward the deer trails that follow the river bank. For some reason, I chose to go off my usual path and bushwhacked through an area of thick brush. As I approached a large crabapple tree, a group of small Hungarian partridges burst out, flying past me. Not expecting to hit one, I halfheartedly let an arrow fly towards the fast moving birds.

Parting the brush to search for the arrow, I located it about twenty feet beyond the crabapple tree. As I pulled the arrow from the ground, something off to my right caught my attention. An old Indian man with long, straight, white, hair was sitting cross legged under a lean-to just big enough to shelter him.

I'd spent a lot of time in these woods since we moved to the farm when I was six, and I had never encountered anyone here before. But then I'd never been at this particular spot before either. This can't be real, I thought. Indians don't inhabit these woods anymore. Recalling that Mohawk people used to hunt in this area, I wondered if he was somehow a remnant from the past who was still surviving here. I was in disbelief, yet my eyes caught his gaze and I froze, staring at him. Although my ears didn't hear him speak, it seemed like I was "seeing" his thoughts in my head. Whatever he was "saying" was soothing and comforting to me. It seemed reassuring in some sense. The message I was getting was "everything will work out okay."

Suddenly a snapping sound to my left distracted me. I glanced towards the sound to see a large deer bounding away. I quickly looked back towards the old Indian. He had disappeared. As I approached the spot he had been sitting I could see the lean-to was made up of a thick low hanging branch on a hemlock tree with brush and chunks of bark leaning up against the branch from the other side.

Although the experience seemed so real, I told myself I must have been seeing things, and I never mentioned it to anyone until years later. However, since that experience I've carried a strong belief that there were old Indians who knew of mysterious aspects about life and the universe that no one else could reveal to me. There were questions I had that would not be answered by my parents, teachers, or the priests or nuns at church school.

For the next three days I hiked and camped in the desert of Monument Valley. This time I was here alone to contemplate my life as it had unfolded since I had first been here years earlier. I needed the sunshine and desert environment to draw the alcohol from my system and clarify my thoughts so I could re-evaluate the direction of my life. The quiet desert landscape, without the distractions of civilization, allowed me to gain an awareness of how my priorities needed to shift now that I was in my early thirties.

Thoughts about my focus and behavior in previous years came drifting back. I reflected on the various influences in my life since my early teen years. The social life in rural northern New York during the early 1960's coalesced around alcohol, which was readily available at an early age. As a teenager I got caught up in that lifestyle, which often led to getting into trouble. Mistakenly, I was under the illusion that I could handle alcohol but, unlike some people, I never seemed to know when I'd had enough. This behavior continued through college and my marriage. Maybe the personal pitfalls I'd succumbed to were part of the learning experience, but if so, when would those lessons sink in? Finally I felt ready to make some changes.

There was no one to distract me from my contemplation during my three days in Monument Valley. I stayed focused on my own thoughts. The only company I had were the little desert lizards that scampered around in a little cave I hung out in. I spent the days walking in the desert, letting the sun pull the alcohol from my system. In the evenings I'd settle in to spend the night where there was a good view of the inspiring rock formations in the moonlight.

Trail mix, sardines, granola bars and water had kept me nourished, but by late afternoon on the third day I was out of food, low on water, and getting very hungry for a real meal. Knowing there wasn't anywhere to get food for many miles if I went back in the direction I had come from, I decided to travel north into southern Utah. I came to the little hamlet of Mexican Hat just before dark.

The little cluster of buildings on the north side of the San Juan River was in the shadows of the cliffs. These sandstone cliffs have eroded into tall spires of rock. Balancing on one of these rock pinnacles is a large stone sombrero, hence the name Mexican Hat. As I crossed the river and drove up into the village I noticed a tavern on the left, actually an old single-wide trailer propped up off the ground and converted to a bar.

I drove on through the hamlet looking for a diner or store, but found no place to get food. Since there was no other place in the vicinity to get something to eat I decided to go to the tavern, hoping they might have sandwiches. Otherwise I'd settle for beer nuts or, better yet, a pickled egg. It was Saturday evening and the parking lot was already quite full. I found a spot towards the back of the lot and backed in. It was getting dark as I went up the stairs of the deck leading to the entrance.

When I walked in I noticed the men's room was directly across from the entry door. Being a trailer, the place was long and narrow, filled with Native men sitting or standing along the bar. I sensed all eyes were on me as I made my way down the bar. I realized that I was in the wrong place with my light hair and light complexion. There was a cold silence and my gut feeling told me that I was in a bad situation. I didn't want to just turn and bolt for the door. Glancing around, I saw that there was only the one door. I needed to come up with a plan quickly.

Attempting to look at ease, I ambled my way about midway down the bar until I found an opening. Stepping up to the bar, I ordered a Bud and a bag of beer nuts. From the mood of this place I was actually surprised the bartender served me. As I gulped my beer down I overheard two rugged looking men in their mid-thirties, about six feet further down the bar. They were talking about me. I noticed they both had long hunting knives hanging from their belts. I saw one of them nod towards me. As I turned my head away I overheard him say to the other, "We're gonna get that guy!"

I could feel the tension in the air. I'd been in enough scrapes before to know when things were serious, and this felt life threatening. It seemed my chances of getting out of the bar were slim, to say nothing of getting out of town in one piece.

Pretending to be somewhat tipsy, I offered some of my beer nuts to the old man sitting to my left. He accepted them without a smile. Then I ordered another beer to give the two bad-asses the impression I was oblivious to their intention. My heart was pounding in anticipation but my thoughts were clear--'make my move now before they grab me.' Taking a swig from my beer, I left a couple dollars on the bar trying to give the impression that I was just going to the men's room. A sober person wouldn't have left money out of their reach in this place. I staggered toward the men's room, which was directly across from the entrance, and opened the bathroom door. Glancing through the crack of the door, I could see that they hadn't followed me and were not looking in my direction. While still holding the door open, I spun around and in two quick steps I was out the exit. Ducking down as I crossed the deck, I got my keys ready as I was crouched and running towards my Jeep.

I jumped in, locked the door, grabbed my old shotgun from behind the seat and put a shell in the chamber. I really didn't want to shoot anyone, but neither did I want the coyotes and buzzards picking through my bones the next day in the desert. I figured if I just took off out of there, they'd spot me leaving and follow me out of the village where they could deal with me in the desolate surroundings. Ducking down in the Jeep, towards the back of the parking lot, I could watch the bar door and hopefully remain unseen. A few long minutes passed before my pursuers came running out of the bar.

They paused on the deck momentarily, looking over the parking lot, like vultures anxiously searching for their prey. Failing to spot me, they ran to their pickup truck and tore out heading north, spiting gravel from their tires.

As soon as they were out of sight I pulled out and headed south in the direction I'd entered the village from. Since the moon was full, the road was easy to see. As I crossed the bridge I shut off my headlights and drove by moonlight. I was nervous and scared, knowing there were no other crossroads or places to hide.

A couple miles south of town I remembered the little canyons east of the highway. When I pulled off the road I quickly brushed out my tire tracks in the sand on the shoulder of the road before driving back into the narrow canyon. About two hundred feet into the canyon I turned the Jeep around facing the highway and pulled up close to the steep canyon wall to be in the shadow hidden from the moonlight. I grabbed a large dark tarp and covered the front of the Jeep, tucking the tarp into the front doors to prevent any reflection. Without many options, I felt my best hope was to wait it out here. I figured they would have turned around after going north for a while looking for me, and would soon be backtracking. This was the only other way out of town that I was aware of.

If things were going to get serious it would happen here. I figured if they spotted me and drove into the canyon I'd try to shoot out their headlights and radiator and then drive past them, out of the canyon to make my escape. I also contemplated a more violent scenario of shooting through their windshield, no matter what the consequences. After a few very long, anxious moments I heard the roar of their pickup and watched as they flew past me going south. The road makes a little sweep away from the canyon I was in. They never spotted me. I threw the tarp in the Jeep and pulled out onto the highway with the lights off and drove north for a couple of hours before pulling over to rest--and to settle my nerves.

Many factors were working in my favor that night. Somehow, I had managed to keep myself in check enough not to panic and bolt for the door too soon, or to take off and try to outrun those two bad-asses. They seemed to have fallen for my drunk act and must have thought I'd be back for my beer and money. They failed to spot me in the parking lot; they didn't notice my vehicle hidden in the canyon. No doubt those two tough characters were pretty baffled about my disappearance that night. Sometime later I wondered if that old hitchhiker I'd picked up on my way to Monument Valley had said a prayer of protection for me when we parted.

The next day while passing through southwestern Colorado, on my way back to Steamboat Springs, I came upon a young Indian family whose car had run out of gas. When I stopped to offer help they were at first very apprehensive, possibly thinking I was going to cause trouble. The previous night I'd been scared by two Indian men. Now this young couple seemed afraid of me. The young man spoke in a manner that suggested to me he hadn't been out in the world much. His wife, who was holding an infant, remained silent the whole time, looking frightened. After siphoning gas from my Jeep and pouring it into their tank, he was able to start his car. Before continuing on my way I gave the young man some cash to enable them to reach their destination.

Chapter Three

Nearly Distracted

I returned to Steamboat, where life was much like being back in college with hordes of single people and almost as many parties. I had good memories of Steamboat. My time there had been socially fulfilling and physically rewarding. The outdoor activities had improved my physical condition and restored my frame of mind.

I'd had a few casual relationships and a couple that were more serious during my three years there. But none of those relationships seemed enduring, except for my involvement with Susan. We had enjoyed a compatible relaxed, off and on connection without serious commitments.

While Susan was spending some time in Europe, I had moved to another part of town and we lost contact for awhile. In the meantime I'd met another woman named Susan, who I'd dated a few times. One evening I answered the telephone to hear, "Hi, it's Susan. I've been thinking of you." We talked for a few minutes, sharing our feelings. When I asked how her brother was, she became rather upset and it was obvious I had mistaken her for the other Susan I'd met more recently. Their voices were so similar. After hearing my muddled apology for the error, she forgave my mistaking her for someone else. We saw each a few times before her work took her back to Europe for two months. We planned to reconnect when she returned. But there seemed to be some other priority gnawing at me which took precedence over any relationship.

The old Navajo hitch-hiker I'd picked up in Arizona that spring had rekindled my memory of the vision I'd had as a teenager. By the summer of 1981 the experience I'd had at thirteen--when I saw an old Indian in the woods near my home--was still haunting me. It seemed like the old man was nudging me to try to find someone who might make some sense of that event some twenty years earlier. I felt moved to pursue some better understanding of it. The only place I was aware of where non-Native people could learn Native American traditions was the Bear Tribe community, an intertribal/interracial group, located in Idaho.

With just under $400 in savings and a vague plan to go to Idaho, I resigned my position at the ski area and said my goodbyes to friends there. During the week before I left town, three women who were co-workers from the ski area came to my home separately, on different nights, to express their affection for me. Their visits took me by surprise because, although we'd become good friends, they weren't women I had been romantically involved with. I was baffled, but I wasn't complaining. There had been so many lonely times in my life, I savored the attention, not knowing when I might be with a woman again. I should have announced my leaving farther in advance.

A few days before leaving Steamboat I posted a note on a local billboard looking for a rider to share gas expenses to Jackson Hole, Wyoming, my first planned stopover. The following day a young woman named Brooke called, sounding excited to get a ride to Jackson Hole where she planned to move in with her boyfriend. I advised her that I only had room for a small amount of gear in my vehicle, but if she could consolidate her luggage I would get her there. As I pulled up to her place the following day I noticed a lot of luggage on the porch and for a moment I considered driving off without her. But then a tall, lovely young lady with long brown hair, wearing a short, bright yellow dress, stepped gracefully onto the porch.

"Hi, I'm Brooke," she hollered. I walked toward the porch, saying, "I just don't have room for all this luggage."

"Oh, please," she whimpered, "I can put some of it in the front seat next to me." Her pretty, pleading smile melted my resistance. While placing her luggage and guitar in the back seat I wondered if I was making the right decision--or just complying because of her attractiveness. With the Jeep crammed full, we set off for Jackson Hole.

After several hours on the road we stopped for lunch at a little diner in the middle of nowhere, Wyoming. After placing our order, the attractive young waitress went behind the counter, rested her head in her hands and stared at me for a moment. It seemed weird and unsettling. She returned with our food, giving me a lot of attention, which made me feel awkward. Her attentiveness towards me seemed peculiar, especially because Brooke was with me. She was either blatantly flirting with me, or just trying to piss Brooke off. But what was even more baffling was Brooke's sudden possessiveness towards me. We had just met a few hours earlier and there had been nothing between us. Suddenly she was acting as if we were a couple, touching my hand, while glaring at the waitress and getting short with her. My impression of Brooke was that she was a classy young lady, with a boyfriend. It hadn't occurred to me that she might be interested in an older, weather-beaten guy like me. What the hell is going on, I wondered.

We got back on the road and continued along that lonesome stretch of land. It seemed as if we were the only people in the world out there, with no other traffic or signs of civilization. With no radio reception we talked and sang songs while she played her guitar. At some point Brooke slid closer to me, took my hand in hers and rested her head on my shoulder. I felt a rush of affection as I caught the sweet scent of her hair and I kissed the back of her hand. Brooke responded by kissing my hand several times and cuddling in close to me. But when she began kissing my face and lips, our affection immediately exploded into passion. I was having difficulty focusing on the road. Brooke was now between me and the steering wheel, so I had to peek around her head to see the road. Just as I pulled away from her to view the road, I saw the first car I'd seen for miles coming around a curve towards us. My Jeep was partially in the wrong lane. Swerving quickly, I managed to avoid the other vehicle, but it scared the hell out me. I pulled over to the side of the road to settle my nerves. We walked down to a little stream to rinse our faces off and refresh ourselves, but again we became aroused. The suddenness of her passion totally surprised and confused me, especially because she'd been talking about her boyfriend and their upcoming engagement. I guessed that our casual compatibility and the lonesomeness of the surroundings had affected her.

When we reached Jackson Hole Brooke said she wasn't ready to see her boyfriend yet and wanted to spend more time with me. My plan had been to camp there overnight and leave for Idaho the next day. She insisted on camping with me that night. We located a campground and set up my pup tent. By now I was having serious doubts about her commitment to her boyfriend and wondering where this thing with Brooke was going. That evening we went out for pizza at a family restaurant and I was enjoying her company. But the family setting there made our age difference really hit home for me and I felt like I was robbing the cradle.

The next day we spent the morning exploring some of the sights around Jackson Hole. I was getting increasingly eager to pursue my journey. Brooke tried to persuade me to take her with along with me, but I wasn't comfortable with that idea. I encouraged her to contact her boyfriend, thinking she would feel differently after seeing him.

Brooke introduced me to her boyfriend when I dropped her off. He was a nice- looking, clean-cut guy who impressed me as being well-educated and more mature than she was. Although Brooke had initiated our little romance, I felt responsible for the situation we now found ourselves in. We agreed to meet later that day, since I still had all her belongings in my vehicle. When I met up with them later, she was even more adamant about going with me. She said, "I need to find out if what I feel for you is real before I can pursue anything with my boyfriend." Her boyfriend seemed resigned to her decision. I figured she was just young and confused; she would no doubt come to her senses once I was down the road.

After a long emotional conversation, we contacted a local minister, named Oscar, who owned a second- hand store in the village. I had been strongly discouraging her from going on with me since I had no solid plan about where I was going or what course my journey might take. She was a very attractive and sweet young woman but, besides our age difference, I wasn't ready to be responsible for her. Oscar agreed to let Brooke spend a few days with him and his wife while she figured things out. We unloaded her gear into his storage area and said our emotional goodbyes.

As I drove off towards Idaho I felt slightly proud of myself for how I had handled the situation. It seemed like I'd done the right thing for Brooke, her boyfriend, and myself. This might not have been typical behavior for me in the past, but something was keeping me focused on my soul's quest.

Years later, in reflecting on this period of my life, I jotted down the following lines:

I hear a whisper deep inside,
a stirring in my soul
I hear a clear voice calling me,
to where I do not know
I hear a song so far away,
I must go seek its source
I know that song from long ago,
I heard it in the forest.

Chapter Four

A White Man in a Native World

My intention was to visit an intertribal/interracial community in Idaho, headed by Sun Bear, an Ojibwa spiritual leader. The following day I located the community and introduced myself to Sun Bear's wife, Wabun. "Sun Bear will be back tomorrow. In the meantime you can bunk with Rick in the big tepee up on the hill," she suggested. Rick was nearly twenty years older than myself. He had left his job with an advertising firm after going through a divorce. Like me, he had come to this community to get a new perspective on life.

The next day I started helping out with chores and getting acquainted with members of the community. When Sun Bear returned later that afternoon I introduced myself and spent a few moments talking with him. Near the end of our conversation he put his hand on my shoulder, saying "I have to leave again for a few days, but we will discuss your path when I return."

The people there seemed to be hardworking and dedicated to the Native spiritual practices. But I was looking for something more, although I couldn't define it. That evening I told Rick about my impatience for meaningful spiritual experiences. This, combined with the feeling that this place wasn't quite what I was looking for, told me I'd be moving on soon.

Rick then told me about an elder who had visited the community a few days prior to my arrival. Rick had been impressed with the old man--a medicine man, he thought. Rick said the old guy had spoken about a spiritual gathering he was hosting at an encampment a day's drive from our present location. Both of us were ready for an adventure. We decided to try to find his encampment and see if we could meet him.

Thinking we might be gone four or five days, I took my sleeping bag, pup tent, and backpack with some clothes. Rick and I set off to locate the gathering. We left my Jeep at an old friend's home in Coeur d'Alene, Idaho and traveled together in Rick's car. I had no expectations, but my intuition told me I would not regret going on this adventure. My knowledge of Native people and their cultures was extremely limited. I was just following an inner voice that called me to search for some answers. I suppose I was now a seeker, without consciously thinking about it in those terms.

By nightfall we were still quite some distance from our destination. We rented a motel room to rest and take showers. Stopping for lunch the next day, we each drank two beers with lunch, thinking we wouldn't have any booze for a few days if we were at the gathering. An hour later we were getting close to where Rick thought the elder was camped. I spotted a small sign at the side of the road which read, "Spiritual Unity Gathering: No guns, No alcohol, No drugs, No cameras." Not knowing if we would be welcome, we left the car at the side of the road and walked up the Jeep trail. The trail wound its way up through a wooded section before reaching a large open, alpine meadow.

About a third of a mile in, we were greeted by a friendly, but cautious Native woman. After a brief chat she pointed us to an older man some distance from us. He was leaning on an old Chevy pick-up, talking to two younger men. She advised that we would need his approval if we wished to be there.

Walking towards him I could see and feel his dark, piercing eyes studying me. His eyes were locked on me and I became aware that he was staring only at me and not at Rick. It felt as though he was looking right through me. There was an intensity and impression of command about his gaze. His eyes seemed to penetrate me like laser beams. His look was somewhat unnerving. A shiver of anxiety went through me, but there was no turning back now.

As I was approaching him to introduce myself, he looked directly at me and said, "You oughta stick around til Sunday." It was early Tuesday afternoon and I had no idea what he meant by that. The tone of his voice seemed to me somewhere between a suggestion and a command. Rick and I introduced ourselves to the elder and the two men with him, who I would later learn were his apprentices. A warm smile spread across the old man's wide face as we clasped hands. He joked with us for a few minutes and his friendliness and gentle demeanor quickly put me at ease. He then invited us to stay around for the spiritual gathering which would begin Friday. He suggested we help the younger men finish constructing the Night Lodge and help with the preparation of the sweat lodges.

I guessed he was in his early seventies, a stocky man of medium height with a broad chest and long torso. He wore his speckled gray/white hair in short braids tucked behind his ears. His eyelids covered all but the shiny dark pupils and his beaked nose protruded nearly over his upper lip. He was dressed in casual working clothes. If I'd met him on the street, I wouldn't have had a clue about who he was. I would soon learn from others at the camp that he was a highly respected medicine man who they referred to as "the Mountain Bear" or, respectfully and affectionately, "Old Man."

Rick and I parted and went off to help two different groups of men working on separate projects. Less than an hour and a half later Rick came over to where I was working and said he wasn't comfortable being the only other white guy there. He'd decided to leave immediately. There was no point in trying to persuade him to stay. I knew he had made up his mind. Since I didn't know Rick very well, it didn't bother me that he was leaving. But if it hadn't been for him, I would never have known about this encampment. I knew in my heart I wasn't ready to leave, although my vehicle and all my possessions were a full day's drive from here. We walked back out to his car where I grabbed my gear and said goodbye to Rick.

Here I was, a stranger in the camp. I had a change of clothes and a little cash. I was a world away from all I knew and all I owned. It seemed I had stepped into another time, another reality. I was suddenly a white man in a Native World. It was a dramatic change from the culture and lifestyle I'd left in Steamboat Springs a week earlier. Never before had I been a minority in a social group. Now I was the only light-haired, light-skinned person at the gathering.

Three sweat lodges were being set up beyond the meadow near the brook. There was a lodge for the women, one for Mountain Bear, and another huge lodge with two rock pits for another elder who would be arriving in the next few days. At this point there were about forty people at the encampment. A large cook tent and another large tent adjoining it, which served as a dining area, were situated near the opening of the meadow. Several teepees and tents were positioned along the north edge of the meadow. The Night Lodge was being constructed near the center of the open area.

Each day more First Nations people arrived, mostly Cree people from Alberta and Saskatchewan and others from tribes in British Columbia. The women prepared three meals a day while some of us younger men worked on the Night Lodge. Others were building a "half-arbor" with posts and canvas to shelter the people from the west wind during certain ceremonies and talks.

Mountain Bear made prayers and tobacco offerings for each tree that would be cut to be used for arbor posts. The older men held "talking- circles" and directed us younger ones with the preparations of the lodges.

Although so many people were working in the heat of the day, I never heard anyone curse or get angry. Everyone participated in making the gathering a positive experience; it was uplifting to be a part of an effort that would benefit all involved. Even the children helped by carrying buckets and jugs of water from the spring to the kitchen tent.

Friendships developed among strangers while we worked on the lodges, gathered rocks for sweat lodges and spent time together in talking-circles. I was struck by the absence of individual ego trips and the strong sense of community that quickly developed. The days and nights that followed were filled with activity. During the next two days we finished constructing the Night lodge, gathered and braided sweetgrass and collected more rocks for the sweat lodges.

In the evenings some of us would play volleyball and another game called cock-fights in which one person rides on another's back while trying to dislodge the riders of the opposing teams. When the teams were chosen I was paired up with a tall, handsome woman named Delores, one of Mountain Bear's granddaughters. Since she was built stronger than me, it worked out better when I would ride on her back, instead of the other way around. It struck me how comical this must have looked to everyone--a blond white guy being carried by a young Native woman as we battled to tip our opponents over. With her strength and my agility we turned out to be a good team and were always one of the last pairs standing.

During the next couple of days I met Mountain Bear's wife, Leanna, and two of his sons and daughters.

Leanna was a very cheerful woman who was quick to laugh and fond of teasing. Even Mountain Bear was not immune from her teasing, although I think she was the only one who was bold enough to needle him. However, he seemed unflappable and laughed off her attempts to rile him. He had an innocence about him, like that of a happy child.

Mountain Bear approached me while I was attempting to shave one morning. I'd run out of shaving cream so I was using cold, soapy water. Lacking a mirror I sometimes nicked my chin or missed a few whiskers. With a serious expression on his face he proceeded to describe his method of removing his whiskers. "When I want to remove my facial hair I use two clam shells to pinch the hairs and then give a quick yank, pulling them out." He grinned. I was feeling the pain of his method just hearing him describe it. Noticing my grimace at his description he broke into laughter. That was his only recommendation that I didn't follow.

Although no one ever asked for money some of us chipped in to purchase rough cut lumber to finish the Night Lodge and contributed to a fund to help with food. Others had brought bulk food supplies to the gathering when they arrived, with everyone contributing according to their ability. I hadn't given much thought as to how much was required to host a gathering of this size, but I now realize Mountain Bear's family must have incurred considerable expense to host so many people. I was glad I had arrived at the encampment early enough to help build the Night Lodge and assist with other projects. It gave me the feeling I had at least contributed towards what was required for the ceremonies and it made me feel I was part of the community, and not a tourist.

A woman from British Columbia invited me for a walk one night to tell me about the night sky and the Great Red Road, otherwise known as the Milky Way. She was an elementary school teacher who taught children of both Native and white families. In an effort to reduce racial prejudices and discrimination she would blindfold the students and ask them to describe a student of another racial identity. Using this and other exercises, she believed the youngsters could become "colorblind" in how they perceived others. Her focus on reducing prejudice seemed to me to be a very positive approach towards improving race relations. It occurred to me that it would be good for all people to be colorblind as to how we view others. Hopefully we could all learn to look beyond skin color, and recognize the spirit of humanity common to each of us.

Apparently the "Old Man" was aware of everything that was going on at the camp, no matter what time of day or night. Although our interaction had been completely innocent, the following morning Mountain Bear informed me that the teacher was married and cautioned me about being alone with a married woman. He then told me about an attractive younger woman who had tried to seduce him while he was visiting an intertribal camp.

Mountain Bear said, "She crawled into my bed and offered herself to me. But I told her I'm a married man and I'm faithful to my wife. I think she was under the impression she would get more spiritual power by having sex with me. I don't know where she got that idea. It doesn't happen like that."

I had met the attractive woman he referred to briefly prior to arriving at the gathering. I wondered if I would have had the integrity under similar conditions to refuse her. I got the distinct impression, however, that he trusted me with some personal information that he didn't feel comfortable disclosing to his family, especially Leanna. I'm not sure why, but over the years I found people were often willing to share very personal information with me.

At daybreak each morning, I crawled out of my pup tent and did a "Sunrise Salute," a yoga stretching exercise I had been doing for a few years. Since no one seemed to be up yet, I felt I could do my exercise without being noticed. As I was doing my "salute" to the sun I spotted a person at the edge of the tree line to the east. Soon Mountain Bear stepped out of the shadows and approached me. I had seen him up when I'd gone to my tent around two o'clock in the morning, and here he was, up and about at daybreak.

For a moment I was concerned that my yoga practice might be out of place in his camp, but when he got closer he said, "That's pretty good!" He told me he was pleased I was honoring the sunrise. He spoke of the sun as a living, conscious being, saying, "He brings life to all things on our mother earth and watches over us every day, sending his light to instruct and warm us." Like most "western- minded" people I had an understanding of the scientific importance of the sun, but had never considered it to be a living, aware being. His concept was more encompassing. In his view everything in our universe is aware and connected to everything else.

As we walked to the tent for breakfast he said, "I've been watching you working on the Night Lodge and helping with the other projects. You're a good worker. You'll make some Indian woman a good husband," he chuckled.

During breakfast he suggested, "How about you help get the sweat lodge fire ready. It would be good for you to sweat with us today." I was very grateful for his invitation and looked forward to this experience with anticipation. Several years earlier I had done a couple sweat lodges on my own, without any real knowledge of what I was doing. This would be my first genuine experience of this Native purification rite. A couple of us spent the afternoon preparing the fire and heating the rocks that would provide the heat in the lodge.

When all was ready Mountain Bear offered prayers to the four directions, to the sky and the earth, and about twelve of us crawled into the sweat lodge. More prayers were offered to all of our ancestors and bowls of salmon and berries were passed around. "Eat some for your ancestors," Mountain Bear advised, "so they can get the essence of the food to nourish them in the Spirit World." Hot, rocks were brought into the lodge, the door flap closed and the old man began the first of four rounds, or sessions, of sweating. Heat and darkness enveloped us as he started singing his sacred songs.

Mountain Bear never left the lodge between rounds to cool off, as most of the rest of us did. At the end of the third round of sweating he said, "I got something I want you boys to hear." Most of us remained in the lodge to listen to what the old man might say. However, just as he began to speak he cut wind and giggled like a school boy, as the rest of us quickly escaped the lodge. This was one of his ways of defusing the tension to an otherwise serious event. When the air had cleared we all crawled back into the lodge for another round. Mountain Bear told us everything belongs to Great Spirit: our lives, our bodies, our health, even our weaknesses and illness, and everything can be taken from us at any time.

Although some of us had been strangers when we first entered the lodge, a bond had developed amongst us through the heat and suffering we shared. The intense heat had melted away our differences, and left us feeling our shared humanity.

As I spent more time with this elder I sensed a man of great personal integrity. He was gentle, kind and good-natured. He brought to my mind the ideal of unconditional love for all people and all beings. There was never a hint of prejudice from Mountain Bear, although he had suffered cruelty at the hands of a Catholic priest at an early age in a boarding school. Like many of his generation he had been punished simply for speaking his native language. However, this enlightened man's consciousness had evolved beyond judgment and separateness. His words and actions conveyed a feeling of sacredness to everything he related to, and he struck me as being a true holy man. Even though our backgrounds were very different I was feeling a real affinity and a growing affection for him. I was feeling more fully alive in his presence than I remembered feeling in my life before. It seemed I could feel the blood coursing through my veins.

There were often occasions when Mountain Bear would talk with me about fasting and other topics. I had to listen carefully and concentrate on his words, since he spoke very softly and in an accent unfamiliar to me. He often stressed the importance of remembering our ancestors and giving thanks and food offerings to them.

"Our ancestors have gone before us into the Spirit World and are willing to assist us. We have to approach them with a good heart and respect to ask for their help," Mountain Bear said. He also placed great importance on fasting in solitude, in the wilderness, as an effective method to bring about healing and gain spiritual gifts and insight.

Mountain Bear said, "It is best to purify our minds and bodies in the sweat-lodge before going on a fast. We need to humble ourselves before the Creator, and ask for the physical and spiritual strength to complete our obligations." Having been raised in a Catholic family I had always been very curious about why Jesus fasted in the desert. I don't recall it ever being discussed or explained during those many years of church school. I was quite ignorant about spiritual practices of other religions and I had not been aware that fasting is part of Native American ways.

Mountain Bear suggested we go for a walk while he shared with me some of the details of his personal fasting--the mountain he fasted on, his routine of fasting for periods of four days and nights without food or water, and his offering of prayers with his sacred pipe several times each day.

When he pointed out the mountain he fasted on I was very impressed with the setting. Even from the base of the sheer cliff it was obvious this mountain commanded an unobstructed view and I could almost feel the many hours of intense sun and heat which would be with him during his days of fasting. I imagined there could also be very challenging cold nights and inclement weather to endure there. I wondered if I could willingly endure the demands of this type of fast.

Mountain Bear told me, "Fasting allows us to quiet our mind and become open to gifts from the Spirit World. It is a time to separate ourselves from the distractions of everyday life and focus our thoughts and prayers on Great Spirit." I believe what he simply referred to as fasting is what many would understand to be a vision quest.

As the two of us walked up a gentle slope near the southern edge of the encampment, he said, "Son, a beautiful woman might appear to you and try to distract you from your purpose. You have to be strong and determined." I flashed on the young woman I had left in Jackson Hole. I was not strong, but I had been determined.

By Friday afternoon, the mood in the camp became noticeably quieter and more focused on the serious aspects of the gathering. There was no more horsing around or volleyball games. More sweat lodge ceremonies were held, so that everyone could purify themselves prior to the Night Lodge ceremony. Others were still arriving from more northern areas of Canada and setting up their tents and teepees. We finished enclosing the Night Lodge, a yurt-shaped, eight-sided structure approximately twenty-four feet in diameter and twelve feet high in the center, with the only opening being a door at the east side. The half- arbor, a semi-circular wind-break made of canvas attached to sturdy poles, was also ready for the opening talks.

Old women were cutting and drying strips of meat on wooden racks in the sun for the ceremonial feasts. It struck me that this could all have been taking place a long time ago. Except for our clothing and cigarette lighters, there was little here to remind one that it was now late in the twentieth century.

Buffalo skulls had been placed at the north and south ends of the arbor, with sage stuffed into their eye sockets and nostrils. Bundles of sage were lit in front of them. The smell of sage drifted through the air, bringing with it a soothing, purifying feeling. As darkness fell more people were arriving, setting up their shelters, and making their way to the arbor.

A fire was lit in the center of the arbor. Some people talked quietly while others sat silently, as more people appeared out of the darkness to settle into the circle for the opening talks. Attempting to leave room towards the center for the Native people, I sat on the ground near the outside of the circle. I estimated there were now approximately eighty adults, plus children in the group. A very large man settled in on my left side, bumping me slightly with his shoulder as he settled in. Glancing his way, I noticed his very stern look. His sleeveless shirt revealed the many skin sacrifices which had left their scars on his right arm. For the first time since I had arrived I was becoming self-conscious about being the only white guy here. I felt like an oddity with my light complexion and hair.

People continued to squeeze tightly into the circle so they could all hear the speakers. When another man wedged in on my right side paranoid thoughts flashed through my mind. Maybe Mountain Bear and those who had been working with me had accepted me, but I wasn't confident those just arriving would.

I jumped slightly when the man on my right elbowed me in the ribs. Then I realized he was offering me tobacco and papers to roll a cigarette. Although I hadn't smoked tobacco for several years I quickly rolled a cigarette to quiet my nerves. I thanked him and he extended his hand. As we shook hands his serious expression softened into a smile which also helped relieve my anxiety.

Soon young warriors came through the crowd with pots of stew which they dished out into paper bowls for each person. I was amazed that there was enough stew to go around since the original pot of stew wasn't that large. It reminded me of Jesus feeding the multitudes with a few fish and loaves of bread.

Mountain Bear stood at the center of the arbor and said, "I'm really happy to see all of you here, and look forward to our time together in our ceremonies and talking-circles." He spoke for a few minutes, welcoming everyone and acknowledged the efforts of those who had traveled great distances to attend the gathering. When he was finished, one of his sons, Elwin, his primary assistant, spoke about their recent meetings with the Hopi elders when they had discussed and compared their respective prophesies. He said, "We were warmly received by those elders and invited into the kiva for our discussion of the prophesies. In our conversations we compared our prophesies, which we found to be very similar. We concluded that mankind has done too much damage to the Earth Mother and we will likely have to suffer the consequences of another Great Purification. Only a major rapid shift in mankind's consciousness and behavior can prevent widespread suffering."

He spoke a while longer before he suddenly pointed into the crowd towards me, saying, "This man with the yellow hair"--all eyes turned to look at me and I wanted to shrink into the darkness, not only because I dreaded being the center of attention, but also because I was feeling more uncomfortable as more people amassed. I felt like I was an intruder into another culture. I feared prejudice and resentment would be directed towards me. As these thoughts raced through my mind, Elwin continued by saying, "He is supposed to be here. He was brought here by the Grandmother Spirits." I was very surprised by what he said. A huge sigh of relief flowed out of me. I silently thanked Elwin and those Grandmother Spirits.

When he had finished, the other elders rose and spoke in turn from eldest to youngest. When the Cree Sundance leader, Many Robes, spoke in his native tongue, his voice seemed to come from the center of the earth. His voice was so deep and strong it reminded me of the guttural rumble I had heard an old buffalo bull make back in Colorado when he was communicating with his herd.

After all the elders had spoken, Mountain Bear asked if there was anyone else who wished to express themselves. Although I had not intended to speak, and was at first not even aware I was speaking, I found myself standing and speaking to the gathering. This was completely out of character for me. I was introverted and usually avoided speaking in public at all costs. Yet here I was speaking to this gathering of Native people. Nervous and uncomfortable a few minutes earlier, I was now confidently addressing my hosts.

Something had come over me. It was like some other force was speaking through me. I hadn't thought at all about speaking, much less what I might say. I don't recall exactly what I said, but the words I heard coming from my mouth were roughly as follows:

"I want to thank Mountain Bear and his family for allowing me to be here at this important event. The kindness many of you have shown me over the past few days is deeply appreciated. Although I know very little about your ways and customs, I believe these gatherings are vital for the continuation of your spiritual traditions. Ever since I was a young boy I've held a strong belief that some Native people possess knowledge and wisdom that can be beneficial to all mankind. I see your coming together here as a way to perpetuate that knowledge and reinforce it in your children so that they might carry it into the future."

Then for reasons unknown to me, I started speaking about buffalo and towards the end of my comments I said, "Just as your people are growing stronger, so does the Spirit of the Buffalo, and in the coming years buffalo will return to populate these lands once again. Thank you for allowing me to express myself." Then, as I'd heard the elders say when they were finished speaking, I said, "that is all I have to say for now."

As I sat down a sudden nervous shiver ran through me. I could hardly believe that I had just addressed the gathering and wondered where those words and the courage to speak them had come from. Later when I told Elwin about these thoughts regarding my speech, he said, "It was a spirit that stirred you to speak and your words arose from your heart, not through your mind." It would be years later that I would learn how few buffalo existed in 1981, and how they have made a comeback since. Their numbers have increased dramatically in recent years, and they now populate areas near the place where we gathered that night.

When the group left the half arbor some of us went to the Night Lodge where we sang and danced circle dances around the drummers. During one of the circle dances a strikingly beautiful young Native woman broke into the circle, to my right, separating my hand from the person next to me. Taking my hand, she squeezed it in hers, as she gave me a long, warm smile. My face flushed at her beauty as I glanced towards her, taking in her big dark eyes, beautiful mahogany face and glistening black hair, which hung in long braids reaching her slender waist.

"I'm Dale," I said, over the drum beats and voices singing. "Kayla," she replied, smiling. We danced and sang to the beat of the drum. I was very attracted to her, but I sensed in her flashing dark eyes that she could be trouble. 'I can stomp on your heart while still smiling at you,' she seemed to communicate. I was also cautious about pursuing a relationship with her, partly because I thought I might be just a "curiosity" for her.

The dancing lasted into the early morning when some of us went to the dining tent for more drumming while we played team gambling games and Kayla continued her own game of flirtation. I finally headed to bed, alone. Some nights I could hear the voices of people singing to the beat of the big drum until daybreak and I wondered if these people ever slept. The beautiful, shrill, haunting sound of the women singing penetrated the crisp night air and seemed to reach up to the stars.

I wondered why all the recent attention from younger women? Was it all about feast or famine, or was I being tested by the spirits in some way? She could have easily been a distraction for me from spending time with the elders. I remembered Mountain Bear's advice to be strong and determined: a beautiful woman may appear to you and turn out to be a distraction. A couple of days later she began spending time with Cal, the handsome Native man who had offered me tobacco at the half-arbor. But a day or so later Cal's head was down and I wondered if he got stomped. Although I could not define my purpose there, it was not about finding a girlfriend.

Carter, a mountain man from northern California, joined the gathering over the weekend with two of his sons. Many years before, he and his family had become stranded and broke while traveling through this area. They were helped and taken in for the winter by some of the Native people living here and had been accepted by them. Carter was not Indian, although with his dark complexion, long braids and buckskin clothing he looked it to me. But Native people always know the difference. It was somewhat comforting to have others at the camp who were non-Native.

On Saturday there was another sweat lodge ceremony led by Henry, another Cree elder. This lodge, the only one of this style I've ever seen, was oblong, with two rock pits spaced mid-way from the center. About thirty of us men participated in this unique sweat lodge.

Later that afternoon one of the Cree men said, "We'd like you to join our warriors' circle for something special." As I walked with him towards a group of about fifteen men seated in a circle I wondered what he had meant by "something special." I no sooner sat down when one of the men handed me a plate of four large raw beef kidneys. Wearing a broad smile he said, "This is our warriors' meal and you are our guest." They all watched with great interest as I accepted my portion and summoned enough courage to slowly chew and swallow the kidneys.

They were thoroughly enjoying this delicacy, dosing their portions with plenty of salt, but were continually glancing over towards me, watching me get mine down. When I had finished my plate of kidneys one of the men asked, "Are you ready for another helping?" "No thanks, I'm full," I said, smiling. Unable to hold back any longer, they broke into howls of laughter, knowing I had not acquired a taste for raw kidneys. They had set me up for their own comic relief and I was happy to have provided them with some laughs. But I was mostly grateful they didn't insist I take a second helping of kidneys.

After they had had their fun with me, one of them told me that Many Robes, who was their medicine man and Sundance leader, had invited me to his circle. I joined the group of men and Many Robes gestured to me to sit to his left. From a distance the quickness of his stride and his tall, lean body had given me the impression he was relatively young, but up close his weathered face and deep, sagging wrinkles revealed a much older man. His white hair was cropped short under a cowboy hat, his nose prominent, but noble, pointed towards whomever he was speaking to.

The elder spoke only in his native language and although I didn't understand his words, his deep rhythmic voice seemed to carry me to another place and time. Many Robes would pause from time to time, allowing one of the men to translate for me. He seemed to have emerged from an earlier time. In addition to his voice, there was something about his essence that always made me think of buffalo.

After a while Many Robes pointed to his sacred pipe, which was resting on a rack of willow sticks in front of me, and indicated to me to light the pipe. After smoking and praying with the sacred pipe I passed it to the man on my left and it went around the whole circle and back to Many Robes, who finished smoking the mixture of tobacco in the pipe. As he knocked the ashes from his pipe Many Robes said something, which was translated for me as follows: "I feel you have a gift for clear dreaming. Remember to trust the messages in your dreams. They will guide you in your life."

For as long as I could remember my dreams had been quite vivid, including color, sounds, smells, touch and even taste. Almost always I could remember at least a few dreams from the night before. I recalled that I had dreamt about several friends and acquaintances just prior to, or shortly after their death. The deceased, even those who were much older, always appeared to be in the prime of their life, and seemed very content. Some I had dreamt about before getting word of their passing. On occasion I'd had other kinds of premonition dreams which typically came to fruition within three days. Could this be what he meant by a gift for dreaming?

Elwin later informed me that Many Robe's sacred pipe was very special and that it was a great honor to be invited to smoke with him. I felt humbled and grateful for their efforts to include me and attempt to share their ways with me.

That evening the men and women gathered at separate fire circles. As I stood towards the back of a group of men who were telling stories and joking around, I noticed Mountain Bear observing me from across the fire. Soon he came around to where I was standing and took a spot to my left where he could speak privately to me. He joked with me for a while, commenting about how men and women had different styles of warming themselves around a fire. "We warm our front sides, while they warm their backsides," he chuckled.

After a little more small talk, without any lead-in, he suddenly stated, "Son, I'm gonna teach you about Indian religion. You got a lot to learn, Sonny, if you want to know about this. It'll be pretty hard. There's a lot of things about it and it takes a long time."

His statements rocked me back on my heels. He'd caught me completely off guard. I was astonished and practically speechless. Feeling awkward and undeserving of his offer, I managed to stammer, "I probably have some things to unlearn also."

"Yeah, a few things," he replied.

Mountain Bear's statement that he was going to teach me his religion was beyond anything I could have imagined. A part of me wanted to learn all I could from him, but I also questioned my worthiness of his attentions. His statement, "It'll be pretty hard, and it takes along time," seemed to indicate this learning would go beyond basic explanation or discussion. It felt like he was conveying the message that he intended to give me a thorough, long-term education.

Why me?, I thought. I was just a clueless white guy whom he'd known less than a week. I glanced around the fire circle, taking note of the Native men in this group who would no doubt envy the opportunity to have Mountain Bear give them personal instruction. But maybe they already had sufficient knowledge. Perhaps it was due in part to my reserved behavior and respect for their ways that he decided to teach me. Possibly because I was a white-man, he felt he could spread his knowledge to a larger audience.

I let go of my mental turmoil and attempted to digest what his words really meant. Mountain Bear then shared a few things with me regarding his beliefs and instructions for the upcoming ceremony. I don't recall the specifics since I was still reeling from his statement about teaching me. After the circle broke up a few of us joined some of the women who were dancing and singing in the lodge.

Chapter Five

From Fear to Ecstasy in the Night Lodge

It was Sunday morning. I recalled Mountain Bear's first words to me, "you oughta stick around till Sunday." Elwin told me it would be a day of fasting to prepare ourselves for the ceremony which would begin at dusk. I was looking forward to attending, although I didn't have a clear understanding of what the ceremony would entail. I assumed it might be something like the sweat lodge without the intense heat.

A couple of young Cree men who had attended his ceremony in the past told me what I might witness in the Night Lodge, but none of their depictions seemed possible to me. They spoke about a spirit- animal that would fly around the lodge, possibly touching us with its wings. They said that other supernatural entities might make their presence known during the ceremony by revealing themselves as sparks of light. These Cree men emphasized that Mountain Bear was a very powerful, highly respected medicine man capable of manifesting awesome events. In retrospect I think what they described seemed too incredible for me to accept at that moment.

Mountain Bear led another sweat lodge ceremony that afternoon and Lance, the big gruff looking man who'd bumped me as he sat down next to me at the opening talk Friday evening, was sitting to my left again in the lodge. Lance stood about six feet four inches and wore a serious look on his face. He seemed very reserved and seldom spoke prior to the sweat.

During one of the rounds a piece of hot rock split and popped off one of the rocks in the pit at the center of the lodge, landing in Lance's hand. When the door flap was raised at the end of the round he showed me the piece of rock, which was shaped like a buffalo. He was so thrilled to have received the "buffalo stone" during the sweat, that he started speaking to me with great excitement. As he opened up, it became obvious he was a kind, gentle soul. Only his appearance was gruff, while his quietness hid his true essence.

After the sweat lodge we sat in small groups listening to the elders. The mood in the camp had become noticeably quieter. Everyone seemed increasingly introspective as we prepared ourselves for the coming event that evening.

We entered the Night Lodge just before dark through the only opening, a door facing east. Mountain Bear and his two apprentices sat at the west side facing the center of the lodge. The preserved body of one of his animal spirit helpers was attached to the wall behind him, but I am not at liberty to disclose what it was. The rest of us sat cross-legged in tight concentric circles radiating from the center of the lodge out to the wall.

When I first sat down, I was at the outer ring of circles, near the wall of the lodge. But as people continued to enter the lodge those of us towards the outer edge moved towards the center to make room. As more people entered and settled in we were packed very tightly against each other on both sides, with our knees nearly touching the people in front of us, our backs nearly touching those behind. There was no room for anyone to possibly move around.

Just as the ceremony was to begin Mountain Bear announced that we were getting some interference, and asked us to use our blankets and jackets to cover any small openings where the lodge walls met the roof. (After the ceremony Mountain Bear told me that word had gotten out to the surrounding area that non-Native people were at the camp and there were some who were opposed to that. He knew who was sending forces to attempt to block the ceremony and told me her name. I had an intuitive sense of who had spread the news about my presence there, although his name had not been mentioned. I'd had a guarded feeling about a man who had been at the opening talks on Friday evening, but I had not seen him since. My gut feeling told me he was the one who had told others that non-Natives were at the camp.)

When Mountain Bear was satisfied that things were in order, he began the ceremony with prayers and offerings to the spirits. The lanterns were turned off and darkness enfolded us. A special sacred song was chanted, used only for this particular occasion. I heard the little bells that were attached to his preserved animal helper begin to ring. My sense of time was lost as we continued to chant repetitive verses. Meanwhile, there were things happening that I was incapable of understanding. I felt the brush of wings around me and saw tiny blue lights flash and move through the air above us. Eventually, I heard the sound of rattles and perceived one to be moving near me.

Suddenly a rattle began tapping me in a slow, rhythmic but gentle manner, going up my right arm, onto my shoulder and systematically, and seemingly purposefully, moved up, continuously tapping, to the right side of my head.

My sense of reality was being shaken to the core. My rational mind knew it wasn't possible for an inanimate object to move without something or someone moving it. I attempted to explain it away as some kind of deception or trickery. Never having experienced anything of this nature, I was skeptical and needed things proven beyond doubt. I struggled to hang on to my reasoning, searching for some rational explanation.

After I'd exhausted the possibility of trickery by

moving my hands all around the moving rattle and was convinced there was nothing holding it or attached to it, my sense of reality collapsed and I involuntarily let out a scream. It wasn't from any fear that my body was in danger. It was more the resistance of my rational mind to what it couldn't explain. The man on my left told me to keep singing. A second later, the rattle still tapping me, crossed to the left side of the crown of my head and immediately my terror turned to bliss. My fear dissolved and left me feeling ecstatic.

Somehow I knew I had received a special blessing from a spiritual power. As the rattle continued tapping me, moving down my left arm my sense of bliss grew even stronger. I did not understand what had occurred, but there was no denying how wonderful I now felt. It was a feeling I had never before experienced. I could not define it, other than to call it spiritual ecstasy. I felt that God had touched me.

I realized this was what Mountain Bear had wanted me to experience and why he had told me to "stick around till Sunday". Since reason could not explain how the rattle, lights and wings were moving about I began to accept that they moved by some unseen forces that I could not comprehend. Although I had not been mentally prepared to accept such events as real, the whole of my being now knew they were as real as the ground I was sitting on. No amount of preparation could have prevented my personal struggle between reason and acceptance of the incomprehensible.

There was no way I would be able to explain these events through any use of reason or logic. It was a mystery beyond my normal human experience and outside the realm of day-to-day realities. I would come to learn that what is important in religion is not rational understanding but the experience itself.

My hunch is that is why Mountain Bear didn't

attempt to explain the ceremony to me beforehand. I doubt if any explanation would have sunk in, due to the lock that rationality had on my mind. He had to blow that lock off before any explanations would be acceptable to my belief system. It seems that some of us cannot accept other possible realities unless and until we are pushed or forced to confront our limited world view--and see that view shattered by some force beyond the boundaries of our currently held reality.

The ceremony closed with a small ceremonial meal. Mountain Bear told various people what herbs or roots they might use for their particular ailments and others what new names the Spirits had given them. I learned that some individuals receive another name when they achieve a new status in the tribe or pass into a new phase of life. I don't know how much time had passed, but I knew we had been in the lodge for much of the night.

People were getting up and moving around and talking, while others were filtering out of the lodge. I stood up and found myself walking slowly, almost mechanically, directly towards the preserved body of the wild being which was suspended on the wall behind Mountain Bear. Some part of my being knew that this Spirit entity was at least partly responsible for my new found state of bliss. There was no intention to my movements. It seemed I wasn't moving out of my own volition. It was as if I was actually being pulled towards the wild creature by some unexplainable force. My eyes were locked on it, and I moved towards it as if in a trance, walking directly between two men who were talking.

I reached out and touched its head and spoke its name. I don't know how I knew its name, but that didn't occur to me until later, when Mountain Bear told me its name. At this point, becoming aware of my actions, I realized I had just touched his sacred medicine, which was probably a major taboo! I glanced over to Mountain Bear who grinned and asked me, "What were you scared of, Son?" I stammered something like, "That was truly amazing! You really blew my mind. It was really incredible"! He chuckled at my amazement, joking with me for a couple moments, which helped relieve my concern about breaking a taboo. I thanked him for the ceremony and started to leave, still in a state of complete awe accompanied by a tired, dazed state of mind.

One of Mountain Bear's assistants caught up with me and told me to wait. The old man wanted to talk with me. I sat down near the center of the lodge and Mountain Bear came over and sat facing me. Everyone else had left the lodge when he turned to me and said, "Son, I'm gonna tell you about what happened tonight." He then told me his spiritual name and the name of his spirit animal helper, the name I had spoken earlier. He said he didn't want those names to be put in a book, because they are sacred names. I don't know why he told me that. I was not a writer and never imagined writing about these events. He explained to me how his animal spirit helper had come to him and how he had prepared certain of its organs, ingesting them during a special ceremony. Through that ceremony he gained a powerful spiritual connection with the being and it became one of his Spirit helpers.

He said, "When we are born, Great Spirit puts a spark of himself in each of us," pointing to his chest. "We are much more than we think, more than a body and a mind, and we are capable of much greater things than we have been told. Most of us have been taught the limitations of what is possible, not what is our true potential. We have a beam of light inside us, the light of Great Spirit. We need to learn how to direct that beam of light."

He went on to say, "I have the gift of leaving my body. When the sacred songs are sung my soul leaves and travels in the Spirit World to get information about how to help people and to get assistance from the Spirits with what I call my 'doctoring' work."

I asked, "Are the spirits you referred to your ancestors"?

"Yeah, and other people and beings from other places," he replied.

"Do you mean other planets"? I asked.

"Yeah, there are some strange things out there. It's really busy out there, lots of spirits whizzing by, going really fast."

Having heard of evil spirits, and curious if they really existed, I asked, "Are all the spirits helping people?"

"Some are not helping in a good way, some cause harm," he replied. I asked him about the blue sparks of light that appeared in the lodge. Mountain Bear told me they were Grandfather Spirits that he had called to be with us to bless us. "They are blessing us and telling us they are here by showing themselves as lights."

He had always spoken to me in English, since I was ignorant of his language, but at some point I realized he'd begun speaking in his native tongue. I interrupted him and reminded him I didn't understand his language. Mountain Bear pointed to his temple, saying, "This doesn't work so good." I understood him to mean that our minds don't grasp certain concepts sufficiently. He pointed his big index finger toward my chest saying, "Son, you will understand it from here, from your heart, the center of your being. Maybe some day you will get it up here," again pointing to his temple.

He proceeded to speak in his native tongue. At times it seemed as if he were praying. Suddenly he ordered me to stand up. "What"? I asked, confused about what was taking place. "Stand up!", he commanded. As he stood himself, I jumped to my feet. He started singing and moving his rattle around my body, his piercing eyes constantly focused on my eyes. I found I could not blink or take my focus from his intense gaze.

After shaking his rattle around me he ordered me to sit again. As he continued in his language I began to have a visual and physical feeling of soaring through space. In this experience I looked over and saw Mountain Bear rocketing through the night sky. My perspective was that I was slightly behind him, off to his right. I felt that I was being carried along with him, that he was ushering me through space. Stars and planets were visible to my eyes as we soared rapidly through the darkness of the night.

Eventually we veered to our right, approaching a pale yellow planet. The journey then either became too much for me to assimilate or too foreign to my experience to register clearly in my mind. Whatever the reason, I don't clearly recall much of the rest of the experience. The aspects of what I could remember were other-worldly.

My next awareness was sitting in the lodge facing him, just as we had been. I had a vague feeling that he had shown me incredible things, but they were beyond my ability to consciously recall. I don't know how long this experience lasted. I was bone tired.

He began speaking again, in English this time, but I was having difficulty concentrating on what he was saying. The extraordinary events of the night, in addition to not having slept or eaten for the past twenty-four hours, had left me mentally exhausted. He was at least twice my age, yet he didn't seem a bit tired and was still trying to help me understand what had transpired. But I couldn't retain or grasp anymore. I told him I needed to get some food and rest. When we stepped out into the morning sun I realized he must have spent several hours with me after everyone else had left the lodge.

This was my initiation into the realm of the Spirit World. The wonderous feelings of true spirituality were something I'd never experienced before. For me it was the most profound and memorable experience I'd ever had.

But for Mountain Bear it was part of a larger reality that is available to us all under the right circumstances. It occurred to me that some Native people accept as natural what the "modern" mind would consider supernatural, if not impossible.

"These things are not just for Indian people, Son," he said, as we walked towards the kitchen tent to get breakfast.

* * * *

At a reunion thirty years later, Mountain Bear's son Denny remembered that my eyes were as big as silver dollars after the rattle had tapped me. He said his dad told him, "One of the Grandfather Spirits touched him to make him a believer."

Chapter Six

The Elders Interpret My Past and Future

At breakfast that morning Mountain Bear told me he had recently visited Rolling Thunder while on his way back north from their (his and his son's) visit with Hopi elders. Rolling Thunder, a noted Shoshone Medicine Man who headed an intertribal camp in Nevada, complained to him about severe pain in one of his ears. Mountain Bear said they went into the lodge to do a healing. He said, "Rolling Thunder was very surprised when the rattle moved through the air and gently tapped only his problem ear, because he hadn't told me which ear had been giving him pain. He was also very grateful for the immediate relief of the pain."

Mountain Bear chuckled, recalling Rolling Thunder's amazement. After my experience the previous night I could understand Rolling Thunder's astonishment. Mountain Bear's humility was remarkable. He never claimed personal credit or bragged about his abilities or accomplishments. He gave all credit to the Spirits.

After our breakfast Monday I went to my tent to rest and absorb the awesome events of the previous night. My body was tired, but my mind was churning. The sensation of spatial traveling I'd experienced as Mountain Bear had ushered me through the night sky brought back the memory of being out of my body when I was fourteen.

* * * *

In the spring of 1961, while riding my bike home from the local fishing pond, I was struck by a fast-moving car on my left side and was thrown into the air. The back of my head smashed into the windshield. I lost consciousness as I sailed over the car and landed in a ditch. I remember looking down from a great height and seeing my body lying in the ditch by the road. I became aware of "myself " floating far above the scene in a misty form, roughly the shape of my body. My awareness of my essence or soul had the shape of my body but it was not well-defined. Then I realized my sense of visual perception had expanded to 360 degrees.

My first thought was, "I'm dead." Then I thought, "No, I'm not dead, but I'm dying." I felt no fear, sadness, or attachment to my body. It seemed to be simply a fact: my body was lying in a ditch and my life as I knew it was over. An instant later, I saw three beings wearing hooded robes. They hovered in the air just above me. I took them to be ancestors or saints. Intuitively, I knew they were spiritual beings. Their backs were towards me as they each spoke in turn, as if they had heard my thoughts.

The first said, "No, it is not your time yet." The second said, "You must go back." The third said, "There is something else you need to do." My soul must have immediately returned to my body. I briefly regained consciousness back in the ditch. I recall seeing an ambulance and asking for a Kleenex. My next awareness was waking up in the hospital and seeing blood on my pillow. I looked up to see my parents and a priest praying at the foot of the bed, as the nurse was cutting off my rubber boots.

Hospitalized for ten days, I was not allowed to move or sit up. My left shoulder and hip were badly bruised and my ear drum had been ruptured. Initially they thought I had a fractured skull, but concluded it was a severe concussion. I thought my experience in the ditch was unique to me until years later when I heard similar stories from others who referred to them as "out-of-body," near-death experiences.

As a result of that accident I was left with a conviction that consciousness survives the body and that we have awareness in the afterlife. It removed any doubt about individual conscious existence beyond the body. The experience gave me a solid belief in a realm of spiritual beings that awaits us when we die. These are not new ideas, of course. But for me they were a personal revelation. In retrospect, I see the accident as a gift which eventually put me on a path to seek something other than the ordinary. The event had changed my attitude about death. I no longer considered death as an end to life, but as part of a continuing process of the soul.

Although those convictions stayed with me, I certainly didn't take up a spiritual path at that time. I had the attitude of "carpe diem," live for the day. It seems I pushed the spiritual aspects of the experience to the recesses of my mind. I didn't walk around thinking about the three spiritual beings who greeted me or about what I needed to do before leaving this world.

I did become more interested in religion and philosophy. While recovering that summer I read essays by Plato, Aristotle, Socrates, and Lucretius that somehow found their way onto my bedroom bookshelf. While I doubt if I grasped much of their writings, they did bring new perspectives to my understanding of life. "On the Nature of Things," by the Roman poet Lucretius, was very thought- provoking. I was particularly impressed with the modernity of his assertion that "no matter is created or destroyed." However, from my experience of my consciousness being separated from my body, I disagreed with his belief that the soul dissipates with the death of the body, at least not immediately.

That summer I visited the Lincoln Memorial in St. Louis, Missouri, and was deeply moved by the display of massive head mounts of buffalo bulls in the entry way.

Those mounted heads spoke both of their majesty and of mankind's disregard for species including, too often, its own. I thought how sad it was that this once great and abundant creature might someday be only available to us as a memory. The experience left me with a lingering concern for these magnificent beings.

The next afternoon Denny came running over to me and told me the elders were waiting for me to join them in the Night Lodge. He gave no hint of what was going on. I entered the lodge with some apprehension. As my eyes adjusted to the dim light in the lodge, I saw Mountain Bear, Many Robes, and the other elder, Henry, sitting near the center.

"Sit down here, Son," Mountain Bear told me, pointing to a space next to him in the circle. He'd always called me Son, or Sonny, which I had taken as a generic form of address towards any younger guy. But I was starting to feel his use of term was taking on a more personal meaning. After smudging me with the cleansing smoke of burning sage, Mountain Bear lit a braid of sweet grass which he waved around us, while praying in his language. Mountain Bear then said, "A certain power has brought you here. We see something in you." He went on to say, "You have a 'good one' (a good spirit?). It was not by accident that you found your way to this gathering. It was directed by the Spirits."

He then said they wanted to help me see the path of my life. He then lit his sacred pipe, smoked and prayed before passing it to me. After we had all smoked the sacred pipe, he said that we are going to sing some songs for you to help interpret your path in life. "Maybe you will get some insight from these songs," he said. They each sang a song for me, after which they explained to me what the song was about.

The first song took me back to my childhood. I

saw myself jogging along the trail through the cedars and hemlocks near the river where I had spent much time as a young boy. Henry told me, "That was the tree song. I sense you have a strong connection to trees." My earliest memories are about sitting under the large old maple trees that lined the edge of our yard when I was three years old. A few years later when I was seven or eight I began exploring the deer trails that followed the river bank about a half-mile from my home. During those excursions I sensed voices from the forest which taught me a chant to repeat as I ran along the deer trails.

The second song was familiar to me because it was the one that had come to me when I was jogging along those trails. As a youth, the chant seemed to give me greater endurance. I felt I could continue to run as long as I kept up the chant. When I shared that fact with them, I was told that nature spirits sometimes give a song to a child that is open to receiving it in order to be helpful to them at times. Henry said, "That song is the wolf song. The reason you could run for long periods is because the wolf has such great endurance."

After the last song, another animal spirit song, Henry, who spoke the best English, looked at me and asked, "Well? Anything?" Not sure what he was getting at, I simply said, "No, nothing."

It seemed that there was a power or force of some kind coming through their songs. But although I had felt transported back in time to the trees and the woods of my childhood, I felt Henry was expecting an immediate revelation of some kind. I sensed that Mountain Bear and Many Robes were coming from a more patient place than was Henry. It was as if their songs included a mystery of some kind that would eventually be revealed to me. I thought perhaps I was supposed to have had some great vision or insight from their singing. I felt deeply honored by the interest they had taken in my life and path. I thanked them for the gift of their songs and their interest in my life.

Many Robes filled his sacred pipe with his traditional smoking mixture, lighted it and passed it around. As I puffed on the sacred pipe, I suddenly recalled what had motivated me to seek out these elders in the first place. It was the experience mentioned earlier of seeing an old Indian man sitting under a lean-to when I was thirteen. It seemed that experience had been with me through the years. But it was taking on a much deeper meaning now. I now knew that the "vision Indian" has been a guide in my life, giving me a nudge and a pull back to nature. It was because of him that I sought out Native American spiritual leaders.

Now, twenty years after that vision, I was sitting with these wise old Native men, having the experiences my soul had called me to. I then told them the story of my vision of the old Indian I'd had when I was thirteen. The elders each spoke to me a while longer, with Henry translating Many Robes words for me. The specifics of their words has been lost over time. I had been unable to grasp why these respected elders were giving me such focused attention. But Mountain Bear's statement, that they saw I had a "good one" with me and that my being there had been directed by the Spirits, helped give me some understanding. It seemed to me that I had finally found the "old Indian" from my boyhood.

The next day I was summoned to join the elders in the lodge again. They were attempting to salvage a severe alcoholic from his addiction. At first I questioned why they wanted me involved in this effort. Perhaps they knew I had some personal knowledge and experience with the problems alcohol can cause in our lives. Although I'd done my share of drinking and consumed a few beers most evenings I never considered myself an alcoholic. Maybe they wanted to expose me to a variety of healing situations. During this session they asked me to give my input and advice to the alcoholic to support their efforts.

Oddly, this was the first time I'd gone without a beer for over a week in a long time, but I neither thought about it or missed it. There was too much going on here to even think about drinking. I was sober, but high on life, and more fulfilled than I could ever remember being. I did contribute some of my personal insights as to how problematic drinking can be in our lives, but I had my doubts about any effect that my input would have on the man's behavior. However, my presence at this healing might have had a positive influence regarding my own future involvement with alcohol. Perhaps when they were 'doctoring' the Indian man some of that healing landed on me as well. The realization of that positive effect would only come to me months later.

I was so engrossed in this Native World that I hadn't given any thought as to how long I would stay at the encampment or how I would get back to my Jeep and belongings. Mountain Bear's initial invitation was for me to "stick around till Sunday," but with each new day there was something the elder or his sons wanted me to participate in. My involvement in their Native World had truly struck a cord within me and I was completely swept up in it. For the first time in my life I felt I was a part of something larger than myself. Although I was the "yellow hair" amongst the Natives, it was satisfying to be part of a group of spiritually focused people, who sought to bring about a better world through their ceremonies and prayers. Hopefully I was giving something of value to the group, even if it was only my support and validation to their ways. I sensed that it was important to Mountain Bear that I stay there longer, not for his benefit, but for my own spiritual growth. I was in awe of him and his abilities and still restrained in my relationship with him. But the joy and excitement I felt being in his presence outweighed my insecurity.

His life seemed so complete as a respected healer and spiritual leader who served his people, while having raised and supported a large family. In contrast, I was a loner, serving nothing except my own needs and desires. Mountain Bear had attended school only through fifth grade, yet he knew more about human behavior than I could hope to grasp, let alone embody.

By the end of the week following the Night Lodge ceremony Carter, his sons and I were among the few that remained at the encampment and Mountain Bear gave me even more of his time and attention. He seemed to have taken a real interest in me, always sitting directly across the table from me at meals, and taking time to tell me stories and legends about his people. The old man seemed to study my every movement. He noticed I had a habit of stretching my arms out to the side after I finished eating.

"You shouldn't stretch like that on a full stomach, Son," he told me. "You could strain your stomach muscles." Mountain Bear gave me advice on a range of topics, including being aware of what thoughts I allowed myself to dwell upon. He said, "Any thought about ourselves or others which is not positive should not be held in our minds. Those ideas can take hold of us and can only bring bad results. They should be sent away."

He demonstrated how to send unwanted thoughts away by moving his open palm in a perpendicular position across his chest from right to left. I had noticed that Mountain Bear never seemed to get angry. On the contrary, he always lifted the mood of those of us in his presence. Although I believe I absorbed most of what he shared with me, some of that information lies beyond conscious recall. It is like silent internal knowledge that only surfaces when it is required or brought to mind. By now I felt that we were developing a heart connection.

Chapter Seven

Finding The Spirit Rock and The Buffalo Bones

Wanting to explore some of the local terrain, Carter, Mountain Bear's two assistants, and I drove up into the mountains to a trailhead leading into a wilderness area. From there, we hiked along a riverbed, following it upstream, and climbed the rocks along the side of a beautiful thirty-foot waterfall. Above the falls the river was wider and quite shallow. I was drawn to walk on ahead of the others, making my way up the river bed while they lingered at the falls.

Where the river bent westward, something called my attention to one of the thousands of rocks that covered the river bed. I don't know what drew me to one particular flat rock about eight inches in diameter. It was under a foot or more of water and was at least six feet to the left of my line of travel. As I lifted the rock from the river bed, I was amazed to see that it had been shaped by nature into a perfect image of Mountain Bear's animal spirit helper. I immediately felt a surge inside of me. There was no mistaking what this was: the details on the rock were so perfectly shaped on both sides I wondered for a moment if human hands had chiseled it. But I realized that it had to have been shaped by forces of nature. Besides, we were so far into the wilderness it wasn't possible that someone would have placed it here. I stuffed the rock inside my shirt, and when we were back at the vehicle I showed it to the others. Amazed at the image, and sounding somewhat envious, Carter asked, "What are you going to do with that?" "I'm going to give it to Mountain

Bear," I told him.

When we returned to camp I went directly to Mountain Bear and gave the "image rock" to him. "Looks just like one of them things," he said grinning. He quickly put the rock in his jacket pocket, shook my hand and headed towards his tent. From his actions I knew he was very excited about the rock and I felt that he might put it with his medicine bundle.

Three weeks had now passed since I had arrived at the camp. The nights were getting cold and Mountain Bear had expressed concern that I didn't have a warm jacket. When he found out I was planning to hitchhike to a town 60 miles from there because my driver's license was expiring, he told me that he had to travel to that town to do some business and asked if I wanted to go with him. I believe his "business trip" was actually an excuse to give me a ride on those seldom-traveled roads. He knew I could get my license exchanged there and he probably knew he could find me a warm jacket in the village.

With one of his sons driving, Mountain Bear, Leanna and I headed for the village. When I left the motor vehicle office the old man was waiting for me and took me into a used clothing store where he showed me a warm, canvas navy jacket priced at one dollar. The jacket fit me perfectly and kept me warm on those cold nights. Because of its connection to Mountain Bear I still treasure it. From there they took me to an old, abandoned boarding school which he had attended through fifth grade. We entered the bleak building and he showed me the small broom closet in the back of the second floor, where he had been put for speaking in his native tongue. He told me how cruel the priests had been to the Indian children. This introduction to Christianity was negative in the extreme. I wondered how and why he was not angry or prejudiced from these early life experiences with white Christian culture.

Later that afternoon they took me out to an old "buffalo jump." Mountain Bear explained that before his people had horses, his ancestors would kill the buffalo for their meat and hides by driving them over a cliff. The buffalo were sometimes lured to the area through prayer or ceremonies. The women and children would slowly begin to move towards the herd from behind, gradually encouraging them closer to the cliff. Warriors who were hiding behind rock cairns along the sides of the bluff would jump up and wave blankets at the buffalo to encourage and funnel them closer to the edge.

This action would cause the animals towards the rear of the herd to start running, which forced those in front of them to run to keep from being trampled by those behind them, thus creating a stampede. From the level plain above, it was a long, steep drop to the base of the cliff where the buffalo landed. As the buffalo tumbled over the cliff, warriors waiting below would kill those that were injured, but had survived the fall. They would spend whatever time it took to remove the hides. cut up the carcasses, and preserve as much meat as they could for the coming winter. He said this technique for hunting buffalo ended after the coming of the horse to their people, which allowed them the freedom to ride out after the herd, and hunt them wherever they were found.

After sharing that information Mountain Bear said, "Go up there and gather some buffalo bones." I didn't know or question why at the time, but I now strongly suspect he knew.

Climbing halfway up the steep embankment, carefully picking my steps in the loose gravel, I eventually located a couple small scraps of bone which I held up to show Mountain Bear. He shook his head as if to indicate, 'not good enough,' and pointed me to go further up and to my right. I quickly proceeded towards where he had pointed and spotted a small piece of bone partially exposed from the dirt. As I scraped the dirt from around it a nine-inch piece of lower leg bone was revealed. I turned as I lifted the leg bone from the ground to see him standing a few feet away grinning at me while holding a lighted cigarette in his hand. It jolted me upright. How did he get up here so fast? He didn't appear to be breathing hard from the climb.

It hadn't taken me long to move up to the spot he'd just pointed to, but it was quite a climb from where he had been standing at the base of the cliff. I was in pretty good physical condition, having done a lot of skiing, running, and hiking in the mountains while living in Colorado for the past three years. He was an old man and a smoker. It seemed impossible that he could have made the climb so quickly. But I was so stunned that I couldn't gather my senses enough to even ask him how he did it. I handed him the bone. "That's a good one," he said, looking it over. Satisfied with my find, he handed it back, telling me, "Keep that buffalo bone with you. It might have special meaning for you someday."

When we were back in their van I showed Leanna the bone, which she seemed very pleased with. Then I asked her if she'd seen the "image rock" I'd given Mountain Bear. She nodded and looked straight ahead, as if to say, "we don't talk about those kind of things." I realized I was just looking to get credit for the rock and shouldn't have mentioned it.

My thoughts returned to how Mountain Bear could have gotten up the steep embankment so suddenly. Why did he even bother to go up there? Was he out to blast my convictions of reality again? Could he move his body through some shamanic ability by his intention? There just hadn't been enough time for him to have climbed that far so quickly. I didn't want to ask him in the presence of others.

From there we went to their home in a small

village, where we spent the night. That evening, while in their living room, I noticed an old photograph of a man dressed in traditional regalia. He strongly resembled Mountain Bear. "That's my daddy," he said. "He was a medicine man, too." I could sense his kindness emanating from the photo, and I understood where Mountain Bear's temperament had come from. He went on to tell me stories about his father, but because that information involved personal spiritual information I don't feel it is appropriate to share that private conversation. Leanna and Mountain Bear also shared stories with me about other family members and ancestors, but again I feel the privacy of those conversations should be respected.

A plaque on the wall read something like this: "May my enemy be strong and brave, so if I am defeated in battle I will not be shamed." This statement seemed so foreign to my mind. Where my concern would have been simply to survive the battle, his people's interest was in maintaining their honor, even at the cost of losing the fight. I could see the importance of honor in their culture and the value in their way of thinking. That little plaque on the wall helped me to understand there are very different approaches to life. I realized that these people truly had a consciousness much different and of a higher nature than my own.

Elwin, Mountain Bear's son and understudy, told me the full story about their trip to meet with the Hopi elders that he had first mentioned on the evening of the opening talks for the gathering. He said the car they drove to Arizona was relatively new, but they had a number of breakdowns along the way which had been expensive. When they were ready to return north they were out of money. Mountain Bear recalled a woman from Phoenix had invited him to visit if he was ever in the area. They contacted her and she asked them to come to her home, mentioning that a group of psychics were there and they would be "channeling" spirits later in the day. After a nice meal they went to a large, comfortable room and sat in a circle. Their host said, "Now the psychics will channel the spirits, then you Indians can do your thing." Elwin said to his surprise the non-Indian psychics began to "channel" Cochise, Sitting Bull, Geronimo, and other famous Native leaders, while he and his dad sat quietly listening.

When these renowned psychics were finished, the host asked Mountain Bear to "do his thing." Elwin said his dad told him to put his rattle on the floor in the center of the brightly lit room, which he did. His dad started singing his sacred songs and the rattle began to shake as it rose up from the floor. The rattle proceeded to move around the room gently tapping each of the psychics before making a circle over him and his dad. Then it returned to the center of the room and settled gently back on the floor. Elwin noticed all the psychics were so moved by the experience they were weeping. They began putting money on the floor near the rattle, which added up to the amount he had spent on car repairs and other expenses for their trip.
I could imagine what went through the minds of those psychics as the rattle touched them. No doubt they were humbled and gained respect for Native medicine ways that day.

* * * *

The following morning Mountain Bear asked me to sit in on a meeting with a local banker with whom he was applying for a loan. "I need you to be my secretary to be sure I understand everything clearly," he said chuckling. When we entered the office with the middle-aged white banker the old Indian introduced me. "He's my personal secretary and he'll need to review the paperwork," he proudly stated. The banker looked up at me, his thick eyebrows arched up above his glasses as if attempting to determine if Mountain Bear was sincere. "He wants me to read through everything before he signs it," I assured the banker. We played it up for the banker and I cooperated fully in my role, asking for clarification on a couple of points. I could tell Mountain Bear was getting a real kick out of this situation. He obviously enjoyed having a personal secretary.

After leaving the bank we bought meat and other food staples before returning to the encampment for another week. Although we'd only known each other for a month, my connection with Mountain Bear felt strong. He had taken me under his wing and had become like a second father to me. I was grateful the Spirits had guided me to such a kind, sincere, holy man. He had given me so much, and asked for so little.

The chill of fall was in the air. I had less than eighty dollars left and there was no possibility of finding work in the area. Although I didn't want to leave his camp, I had to face the fact of the coming winter. When the reality of my leaving set in, Mountain Bear and Leanna suggested I build a cabin on their land and stay on there, but a part of me knew it was not meant to be at this time. I knew they would soon be moving back to their home in the village for the winter. It would be a long, lonesome winter here, even if I could somehow manage to get a little cabin built before snowfall and get firewood up, which didn't seem likely considering my lack of finances.

I explained that I needed to get to where I could find a job so I could support myself. They understood my circumstances, but seemed disappointed.

Mountain Bear and Leanna were standing together, waiting, as I approached them to say goodbye. With a slight smile, Leanna extended her hand and clasped my hand inside both of hers. When Mountain Bear shook my hand he pulled me in close, giving me a bear hug with his left arm. Awkwardly, I returned his hug and thanked them for all they had done for me. He said, "Come back and visit us when you can, Son." I felt like I was leaving home. I had to turn away quickly before I choked up with emotion. As I walked away, I felt tears swelling in my eyes and didn't dare look back. It was easy to love these gentle people and not so easy to leave them.

During a reunion with two of his sons, thirty years after my stay at Mountain Bear's camp, we reminisced about my stay there. Denny's memory was impressive. He recalled many details of my experiences at the gathering with clarity and detail. He told me his dad was sad when he realized that I was preparing to leave the camp. Mountain Bear said to him, "I don't want to see that guy leave! I think I'll tie him up and keep him here." It touched my heart to hear that, as I still so many years later feel deeply connected to him. In a way, perhaps he did tie me up and keep me there. I feel part of me is still there, sharing time and life with Mountain Bear.

Chapter Eight

Dreams Infiltrate Reality

I caught a ride with Carter and his sons who were traveling to Northern California through the mountains, stopping to see people he knew in remote places along the way. Although I'd washed my clothes in the stream at the camp occasionally, they needed a more thorough cleaning. When we eventually reached a town with a laundromat we stopped to wash our smoky, dirty clothes and take showers. Carter's buckskins, which had been dark grey from the dirt and smoke, were now nearly white. While at the camp I'd taken sponge baths and dips in the pond to wash off, but my first shower with hot water in over a month was absolutely heavenly. Hot water flowed over my shoulders and ran down my back and chest, its warmth penetrating my skin and soothing stiff muscles. We spent another day visiting other friends of Carter's before they dropped me off at a friend's home in southern Idaho where I'd left my Jeep.

I crossed into western Washington state and then south across the Columbia River, working my way towards southern Oregon. Along the way I took little excursions, hiking mountain trails, to get the feel of the surroundings. I had no specific plans other than to find a job soon, since I was running low on money. There were no thoughts of returning to Steamboat, I wanted to see what life had in store for me next.

I decided to try to locate an organic vegetable farm in Northern California, where Carter had told me I might be able to find temporary work. By the time I got to Crater Lake in southern Oregon I was low on gas and practically broke. With just over two dollars in change left,

I only had enough to purchase an apple and a muffin at the little store there. After setting up camp for the night I searched my Jeep and found a tin of sardines and a bag of pennies in my tool box, which I counted to be exactly three dollars.

The next day I drove into Northern California. I was running out of gas as I drove and coasted along a back road through the mountains. It was a beautiful day and I was in a very optimistic mood even though I was hungry, broke and nearly out of gas. I was singing "I don't give a damn about a green-back dollar, spend it fast as I can". When I saw a "mom and pop" store with gas pumps, I coasted up to the pumps, my car running on fumes. I put in three dollars worth of gas (1981 prices) and took the bag of pennies in to pay.

When I poured the pennies from the bag unto the counter the middle-aged woman minding the store exclaimed, "Oh no!" She was obviously not happy to be getting paid with pennies. "It's all I've got," I said. At first disgusted with me, she lightened up after a while and started helping count out the pennies. By the time we finished she was laughing, amused at my situation and carefree attitude. She said, "Come back again, pennies or not." As I turned towards the door she handed me a sandwich, saying, "Here, this is on me. You might need it."

I made my way along the Trinity River, eventually locating the vegetable farm Carter had told me about. With more than a little persuasion the farmer put me to work in exchange for meals, a place to camp and a little cash. After working there two weeks I went off to visit Carter and his family for a few days. When I returned, the farmer was very grumpy, partly because I'd been away several days longer than I'd planned and partly due to his irritable personality. I figured it was time to move along, but when I was packed and ready to leave, the battery in my Jeep was dead. I asked the farmer to give me a jump start, but he refused, telling me it wasn't his problem and let loose with a flurry of expletives.

In the heat of the day I carried the heavy battery up the long hill to the road, stopping to rest occasionally until I reached the gas station in the little hamlet over a mile from the farm. Leaving the battery to be charged, with my remaining seven dollars I walked to the diner for a "last meal." While eating, I overheard a logger telling the waitress he needed some help cleaning up stumps from a clear-cut in the mountains nearby. I approached him and got two weeks' work throwing broken stump pieces into a caged wagon pulled by a small dozer over steep terrain. The work was very physically demanding, requiring me to walk back and forth across a steep mountainside all day lifting heavy pieces of wood into the cage. But I earned enough to keep me in food and gas for awhile.

When the job was over I made my way back to Carter's camp in the Trinity Alps of Northern California and spent a few days there helping him and his family pack in supplies for the winter on the horses they kept for traveling around the back country. I'd spent a lot of time in a saddle, but never in mountainous terrain. The narrowness of the trails cut into the sides of the ridges was unsettling. One misstep and horse and rider could tumble far down the ridge into trees and boulders below. Fortunately, their horses were calm and sure-footed.

Carter's place was located on a level flood plain below a steep ridge. He and his wife and their two youngest sons had built a comfortable cabin and established a very large, productive garden which was irrigated by a gravity flow system from a spring on the ridge. A few goats supplied them with milk and cheese, ducks and chickens produced plenty of eggs and meat. The family was pretty much self-sufficient except for bulk grains and a few other supplies they brought in on the horses. Their clothing was made from deer hides which they had smoke-tanned. They showed me a family portrait taken in the mid-seventies in which all of them were dressed in hides and coon-skin hats, looking like mountain men from the 1800s.

When I decided to hike out to explore the area for a few days Carter told me I would encounter a community of artists living a couple miles upstream, but failed to mention that some of them were nudists. While hiking the trail along the river, I was taking in the natural beauty of the surroundings of the river valley. Suddenly a lovely, naked teenage girl, with dark hair flowing past her waist, galloped past me on a white horse! If Carter hadn't told me about the commune I'd have thought I'd slipped into an alternate dimension, where Lady Godiva was alive and well. A little further up the trail I came upon some people swimming and sunbathing by a deep pool at the edge of the river. Unaccustomed to seeing people in the nude, I was uncomfortable and tried to avert my eyes to avoid gawking like a voyeur. Two men in the group approached me and introduced themselves as Michael and William. The formality of the introduction struck me as inconsistent with their nudity. Why not Mike and Bill? I thought.

After chatting a while they gave me a tour of their "hobbit"-like rustic village located in the center of their two-hundred-acre private parcel surrounded by national forest. Each individual or family had their own rustic cottage built along the hillside above the river. They looked like very cozy shelters, each one unique, constructed from rocks and trees found nearby. This group of artists and craftsmen had also constructed a large circular community center where they hosted events for other groups of counter-culture folks and shared communal meals. They produced handcrafted articles, such as paintings, woodcarvings and leather clothing, which they sold at fairs or craft shows along the coast. They also grew much of their food and gleaned what they could from the forest.

That afternoon I hiked further upstream and camped near the river. Late the following day I came upon some people building a house on a ridge above the river. While talking with one of the carpenters, a very attractive woman, wearing only a short skirt, introduced herself as Sheryl, one of the property owners, and asked if I was interested in helping with the construction of the house. Still not used to nudity, I accepted the offer, while attempting not to stare at her beautiful tanned bosom. This remote mountain ridge was many miles over rough roads from the nearest store, so the owners provided nourishing meals and lodging for the four of us working on the house. Two weeks later, with some much needed cash, I made my way back to my Jeep which I'd left on a ridge above Carter's place.

From there I went to Mount Shasta where I camped and hiked for a week before meeting up with Carter and his wife who had planned a sweat lodge ceremony near the base of the mountain. After the ceremony, I did a four-day fast further up the mountain.

Prior to arriving at Mountain Bear's camp, I called home to inquire about everyone in my family and let my parents know my whereabouts. They informed me that one of my brothers had suffered a serious eye injury. Concerned for him, but helpless to do anything about it, I had asked Mountain Bear what he would recommend. "Fasting is the best way to help it," he said. "Just fasting"? I asked, "Is there anything else"? "No, just fasting and praying is what's best," he replied. Since fasting was not part of my brother's reality, I decided I would fast for him. (It would be several years before I was introduced to the concept of "standing in" for another in spiritual healing.

Eventually I attended ceremonies were one person would eat for another who was fasting, or ingest peyote for another who was ill.)

The first day of the fast went by without difficulty, but I struggled with hunger for much of the next day and looked forward to periods of sleep and dreaming under the stars. As much as I tried to focus and pray for my brother, other thoughts kept distracting me.

Thoughts about my Catholic upbringing kept swirling through my head. Prior to meeting Mountain Bear, Catholicism was the only religion I had ever been exposed to. Although my parents were both very devout, I had issues with the church. My mother had told me about taking Janis, my younger sister, to be baptized when she was an infant. Since I was only three they brought me along with them. The priest sprinkled holy water on my sister and then asked, "What is to be the given name of the child?" At that point I piped up and said "Peter Wheat," the name of my favorite bread. Mom told me that my dad started laughing, but she was embarrassed. The priest became upset with me, suggesting they should have left me at home.

Like most Catholic children I had to endure years of church school and religious studies under the tutelage of strict nuns and priests. I stubbornly resisted efforts to persuade me to become an altar boy or to join Catholic youth organizations. As teenagers my brother, Dave, and I would go to confession every Saturday so we could receive Holy Communion on Sunday morning. I took it all very seriously and would tell the priest every sin I could possibly think of. Typically, Dave would make his confession before me. Since Dave was an altar boy, the priest recognized his voice and on one occasion asked Dave if I was next in line for confession. When Dave responded that I was, the priest said, "Well, I'd better get my cushion out!"

My thoughts then went to my senior year of high school when I had a very stern, ill tempered, Jesuit priest as instructor for religious studies. During a discussion about limbo, where we were told the souls of those who were not baptized go after death. I asked, "How could a loving God exclude innocent people from heaven and condemn their souls to limbo simply because they hadn't been baptized?" I was referring to people in remote places that had not been exposed to Christianity.

The priest responded to my question by saying, "You're out of here!" He expelled me from class which nearly prevented me from graduating from high school, because I would not get credit for the class. That was the final blow to my connection to the church. If arrogant pricks like him were in charge of our spiritual development I wanted nothing more of it!

While contemplating feelings of guilt I began to make a correlation between consuming alcohol and guilt. Recalling that most of the people I'd known in my home town were Catholic and heavy drinkers, it occurred to me that the Catholic Church's "gift of guilt," which was bestowed on us all in church school, had some role in our behavior. I began to understand that guilt was at least partly responsible for my involvement with alcohol. There seemed to be a cyclical, self-perpetuating aspect to my drinking. The guilt and bad feelings I experienced from consuming alcohol were temporarily relieved by more drinking, which resulted in a hang-over and more guilt.

Although I do take issue with the hierarchy of the church for fostering fear and guilt amongst its followers for the purpose of loyalty and control, in no way do I mean to diminish the positive things many priests, nuns or the Catholic charities accomplish. Nor do I intend to belittle practicing Catholics. These were my experiences and personal conclusions. I am now personally convinced that we can all have a direct connection to our Creator without the need for a priest, minister, or rabbi to stand between us and the divine. Spiritual counselors can be helpful at times in an individual's life but they do not hold the keys to our ultimate destiny. I had gained a sense of spirituality from the mystery of the Mass, when bread and wine become the body and blood of Christ, and was aware the smell of incense and holy water uplifted my feelings. It had given me an understanding that there are things beyond the mundane and that there were methods to communicate to higher powers.

I had distanced myself from Catholicism, but its gift of guilt will probably remain in my subconscious throughout my life. The young mind is fertile ground for any seeds of thought, positive or negative. Once those seeds take root they are very difficult to uproot. They can distort our behavior and self-image. In recent years I've heard the term "recovering Catholic" which seemed appropriate to my life situation.

Sometime late in the second day of my fast, my hunger subsided and I was better able to focus on my intention. My dreams became very vivid and easy to recall, and with no other distractions they would linger with me throughout the day. It seemed I had gotten past the distraction of hunger and was shifting into a different state of consciousness. I focused more on praying for a good outcome for my brother's eye problem. I wasn't confident my prayers would be helpful, but it seemed to be the only thing I could do.

During the third night of fasting I had a very clear, detailed dream about a horse ranch. I saw an image and heard the name of a woman who was central to the ranch operation. This dream felt unusually potent. Although it held no meaning for me at that time, its clarity and force grabbed my attention.

Two days after my fast, I was having breakfast in a diner in the village of Mount Shasta. I struck up a conversation with an older gentleman sitting near me who told me he had recently been working as a landscape architect at a horse ranch in central California. When I mentioned I was looking for employment he suggested I might find work at that ranch, since they were in need of carpenters there. He then told me the name of the woman who was in charge of hiring at the ranch. I almost choked on my coffee. It was the same name that had come to me in my dream during my fast. The coincidental conversation with the stranger about the horse ranch reinforced the feeling that my dream was significant. Recalling Many Robe's advice to trust in my dreams, I got the address of the ranch and left for there the next day, taking the less traveled roads.

Chapter Nine

Almost Paradise

Nacimiento Ranch is situated in central California, west of Paso Robles in a beautiful canyon surrounded on three sides by steep ridges. Fifty comfortable duplex cabins were scattered along the hillside among large old oak trees near the base of the ridges.

Upon my arrival I inquired for Linda, who immediately struck me by her strong resemblance and even her name to the woman in my dream at Mount Shasta. She directed the equine programs. I was hired on as a carpenter/ maintenance person, and received a small salary plus meals and a comfortable cabin to live in. The timing was excellent because winter was not far off. There was little reason to leave the ranch with all the amenities, good food and social life available there.

Naciemento Ranch is owned by Alexander Islinger, animal behaviorist and accomplished equestrian from Germany. Alex's vision was to establish a residential learning center for professional horsemen and trainers. His focus was to promote greater cooperation and connectedness between horse and rider.

The ranch operated as a guest ranch and teaching facility for advanced horsemanship with additional programs for personal development. In addition, the ranch offered programs for personal insight and life changes. The main focus of the business was instructing resident students in advanced horsemanship and teaching alternative healing methods for horses with injuries and behavioral problems.

The secondary focus was the offering of human development classes in yoga, Feldenkrais Movement, and meditation. Other new age workshops and seminars were offered in conjunction with Esalon Institute of Big Sur, California. Although I knew a few yoga stretches I'd learned from a book in the mid-seventies, this was my first exposure to "new age" philosophies and the internationally known leaders who came to the ranch to conduct workshops. There were sport psychologists, among others, whom I found to be effective and deeply involved, while some of the presenters impressed me as being shallow and self-serving. The difference between them and Mountain Bear was dramatic. While he was authentic, and powerful, yet humble, some of these presenters demonstrated plenty of self-importance, but lacked substance.

The large dining hall was staffed by two professional chefs who prepared three gourmet meals daily. Semi-formal dress was required for the elegant dinners. Carafes of wine were set at each table. Other facilities included a conference/recreation building, library, tennis courts, a swimming pool, hot-tub and stable. There were pastures and paddocks for forty horses, a stable with box stalls, a quarter mile track, and a riding arena. There were also many miles of riding trails along the ridges surrounding the canyon.

Most of the resident students were women in their twenties and early thirties from Germany, Switzerland, and California who were there for six months to a year. I enjoyed the camaraderie of the students and guests and made close and lasting friendships with several people I met there.

Life at the ranch gave me exposure to ideas and people of different backgrounds. Mornings began with meditation offered at 5:30 A.M., after which I'd go for a run on the horse track before breakfast. Classes in yoga, Feldenkrais Movement or other new age offerings were held late afternoons. On occasion after dinner we would dance for hours before retiring to our cabins. We went out for trail rides on the ridges every full moon and sometimes rode up to twenty miles on days off. Occasionally there were two- or three-day trail rides with overnight camping. While living at the ranch I was given an Arabian gelding that was too spirited for his owner. However, with some effort, he became a very reliable mount and eventually I passed him on to a Native friend when I left the ranch.

Tom, a contract landscaper at the ranch, was a rugged individualist in his mid-thirties. He lived in a cabin on an old ranch in the mountains ten miles south of Nacimiento Ranch. He had a couple of mustang horses he'd purchased as colts and was training to compete in endurance "ride and tie" events. We would go on long, demanding rides to condition the horses and to get a workout for ourselves. Tom had a reputation for putting his friends through demanding trials to test their abilities and determination. He always pushed me to my limits. It was a real challenge for me to keep up with him.

Even though we were both loners, we enjoyed each other's company from time to time, whether on a trail ride, running on mountain trails, or philosophizing about life, women or horses. We became good side-kicks as kindred spirits and had many good adventures together. He was like a true brother and I will always treasure our friendship. We stayed in contact for years after I moved from the ranch. I would visit him whenever I traveled through that area.

While at the ranch I kept in touch with Mountain Bear through letters for several months and told him about the fast I did on Mt. Shasta. In his reply he expressed sincere interest in my fast and encouraged me on my path. Unfortunately, Mountain Bear passed away a few years later. Although I never got to see him again in the body, he is with me in my thoughts and dreams. Meeting and spending time with him was truly one of the greatest gifts to my life.

Being at Mountain Bear's gathering had changed me, but I wasn't fully aware of the extent of that change. However, I realized the experience had yanked me out of my self-focused mentality and instilled in me a greater sense of connectedness to a larger community and the awareness of a much larger reality. For the first time in my life I felt some responsibility for the welfare of others and humanity as a whole and gained an appreciation for giving in return for receiving. I became aware that my desire for alcohol had diminished substantially. I had gained a deeper respect for women from my observations of their nurturing, stabilizing presence at the gathering. These wives and mothers were strong, capable, self-confident individuals. Their self-worth was based not so much on their physical beauty, as I'd witnessed so often in my own culture, but in their personal strengths and contributions to their families and the tribe.

Chapter Ten

Entering the World of Grandfather Semu

I'd been at the ranch nearly eight months when I heard about a conference in Ojai, California featuring Rolling Thunder, the medicine man from Nevada whom Mountain Bear had spoken of. Due to Mountain Bear's influence on me I wanted to learn more about Native American spirituality. I made plans to attend the conference. Although I wasn't especially drawn to Rolling Thunder, there was another elder present, a Chumash medicine man, Semu Huaute, known to many only as "Grandfather." His wisdom, sense of humor and apparent lack of prejudice impressed me. After listening to this old man speak, I found an opportunity to talk to him during a break. He invited me to visit his place on a mesa in the Cuyama desert, about three hours southwest of the ranch.

Following the directions he'd given me I headed for his camp the following Saturday evening. As I turned off highway 101 and headed southeast through the foothills a heavy fog gradually settled onto the landscape mixing with the blackness of the night. Nothing was visible. The fog and darkness created a feeling of mystery; I felt I was in another dimension. My Jeep and I could have been floating through a mist in space. For a while I was not at all sure of where I was until an owl glided past my windshield, which reminded me of Grandfather, knowing he was of the Owl Clan. A half-hour later another owl flew across at an angle in front of me, bringing the awareness that I was near the turn off. Soon I spotted a small red flag on a fence post at the side of the road, the marker for the jeep trail to Grandfather's camp on the mesa. The dirt tracks left the road and went along the edge of a field for a half-mile to the Cuyama River, which is usually shallow enough to drive across. I drove to the river bank. But the river was running high, too risky to cross in the darkness. I could smell the junipers in the air and like the fog I drifted into the night.

When I crawled out of my sleeping bag the first rays of sunlight were stretching out over the high, flat mountain wall. I was standing near the edge of a long, wide valley separating the mountains from the desert. A mile or more to the south pink/tan cliffs rose straight up from the foothills. I walked to the river to check the depth, looking for a safe place to cross. The riverbed shifts somewhat depending on the rainfall in the mountains so each crossing is different. After finding a spot where there weren't any deep holes I gingerly drove out into the river avoiding big rocks and carefully picked my way to the other side. After negotiating my way across the rocky river bed I was at the base of the mesa.

On the north side of the river the jeep trail goes up through a narrow notch in the mesa wall and climbs up to the top of the mesa overlooking the Cuyama Badlands. The mesa is over a mile long and relatively flat, with higher rises on the north side climbing towards the mountains. The steep walls on the south side dropped off to the river bed. Juniper trees, sage and other desert plants covered the landscape. The dirt tracks continued another quarter-mile before reaching a rough cabin with a dirt floor that Grandfather Semu and his wife, Eneke Alish, called home. It was early Sunday morning when I knocked on their cabin door. Grandfather invited me in and Eneke Alish brought us coffee.

Two walls of the cabin were covered with wooden shelves which held dozens of large glass jars containing various herbs, roots and berries. Eight or ten small chairs were set in a circle, surrounding the open center of the cabin. Grandfather's chair was near the back wall facing the door. The smell of juniper wood burning in the woodstove mingled with the refreshing smells of sage and other herbs that hung from the rafters.

They had a small garden, twenty some goats in a large fenced pasture and a bunch of chickens. I was struck with how happy and content they were with so little in the way of modern conveniences. In addition to three of his grandchildren, two other couples and their children lived on the mesa in their own shelters.

Grandfather was then in his mid-seventies. He had grown up in the old ways and traditions, but also had interacted with mainstream society since grade-school and had an understanding of both worlds. The term "grandfather" is used to show respect for a learned elder and his name, Semu Huaute, means brave, wise like the owl. He had been a heavy-weight boxer when he was younger and his strong build and powerful presence commanded respect.

Grandfather had a strong, deep voice and a good command of the English language. He had a keen memory and his fantastic sense of humor could always lighten up the mood. Those who spent much time with Grandfather knew him to be a healer, a seer, and a medicine man. I would eventually learn that many people who had known him for years were in awe of his abilities and knowledge. They had witnessed many mysterious things that happened in his presence. Rather than taking credit for those mysterious events, he would simply chuckle and say, "I don't pretend to know anything or do anything. I'm just a master of coincidence."

Grandfather was a good psychologist without formal training. He had only a fifth-grade education before leaving school. However, he had a deeply rooted instinct for psychology from his traditional upbringing as well as much life experience. Being a wounded veteran, he understood the horror of war and its effect on the human psyche. He did not seem to judge people, but recognized we are all products of our culture, experiences, and family upbringing.

He said, "I don't prescribe any herbs or remedies, as prescribing could have legal consequences. But I tell people that if I had their problem or condition, I would take such and such." He always seemed to know what was troubling people without asking. Being a seer he seemed to know a lot about people at first glance. For example, he knew immediately upon seeing a person if that individual was using alcohol or if a woman was in her menstrual cycle.

Grandfather was also a history buff and seemed well-informed about European and American history. He had also read the Christian Bible and would occasionally quote passages to make a point of comparison to Indigenous beliefs. In all my time in Grandfather's presence I never heard him speak critically or negatively of other individuals. However, he was critical of institutions such as organized religions and government. Grandfather always spoke highly of Jesus, but felt Christianity had strayed far from the message he brought to humanity. He believed many Christian denominations were more concerned with their own financial strength and political power than with pursuing Christ's teachings of "Do unto others as you would have them do unto you."

He had a unique perspective on culture and society and a broader perspective of current events than I had encountered in Western culture. He believed that all races and cultures of the world had positive aspects to share and that we should find ways to co-operate and combine knowledge.

I would eventually spend the better part of ten years closely associated with Grandfather Semu. As we grew closer over time, he eventually adopted me as his son, giving me a medicine pouch and Chumash name. During those years I spent many evenings with Grandfather, listening to his stories about medicine men and women he had known and their abilities and healing techniques. He was always willing to answer any questions myself or others asked about Native spiritual practices. Grandfather also related many legends and traditions of the Chumash people, and explained how those traditions prepared the children to become valued members of the tribe.

During one of my visits I found an old trunk in a storage shed filled with his personal papers, birth certificate, and old photos, which he gave me permission to go through so I could get a full picture of his personal history. Reading in one of his notebooks I saw he had written, "I am not a holy man. I am a seer, a healer. I am just a man, and I make mistakes like any other man." Regarding healing or medicine work he said, "I am just a man. When I do healing something comes over me and I know what to do and when I need to do it. Having good thoughts towards others is like a prayer for them. It's good medicine."

Curious as to what led him to become a medicine man I asked Grandfather one evening while we sat in his cabin if he would share that information with me. He sipped from his coffee cup, then he spoke as follows: "The elders would observe the children and look for signs that told them what the children's inclinations were. They saw that I was compassionate with the elders and with animals, so I was selected for training in the ways of healing. With my parents' permission, I was taken by some of the men and put in a small hut in the center of the village where I had to stay for several days. The elders would bring me enough water to rinse my mouth and then give me a sip to hold in my mouth until they returned, after what seemed a very long time. They would check to see if I had swallowed the water, which I could not or I would have failed this first test. I would have to spit the water out into a bowl they brought. Then I was given fresh water and had to repeat this process for several days. I was allowed no other food or water during this time. Next I was taken on a long walk in the desert. I carried a heavy rock to build endurance and again I had to hold sips of water in my mouth for long periods without swallowing it."

Although he attended school through the fifth grade, each summer he was returned to the elders for more tests and training. When he reached adolescence he and the other boys that age were taken by the elder men into a darkened lodge and given datura (Jimson weed root which had been ground into a powder and mixed with water). Grandfather said his was the last generation of his tribe to be given datura. "I don't know anyone who still knows how to properly prepare it and supervise its use," he said.

"All the young boys of the tribe went through this, not just those of us who were being groomed to be healers. We were to drink this medicine down all at once, after which we would spend four nights and days in the lodge to have our visions of what our life work would be. The medicine would show us what we were to do in life. The elders would check on us periodically during our stay in the lodge."

"Datura is very dangerous and nothing to play with! You must be instructed and prepared for it and the plant must be handled properly. The root needs to be dried for a year before it is used. Each part of the plant has different qualities or powers. It is mashed into a tea and you drink it all at once. You feel it in your feet first, then it erupts up through you, and when it hits the top of your head you feel an explosion. It feels like you were hit in the back of the neck with a sledge hammer. It almost kills you.

In a way you are dead and if you don't vomit you will die. You travel for four days to many strange places and learn that specific knowledge of things will be available to you when you need it. You see strange beings and people. Datura was typically taken only once in your life." Grandfather went on to tell me some of his own experiences under the influence of datura.

"Were there other ceremonies or experiences that were part of your training, Grandfather?" I asked.

"As an adolescent my training continued under the supervision of the elders." He said, "I was taken into a cave and slowly they would teach me and let me experience things unseen, so (I was told) *you would not die of terror when you get older and go into these experiences by yourself.* The elders would call the forces to come into the cave so you could learn that there are powers that you can feel and see the effects of, but could not yet see the powers themselves.

"At first it was frightening to be touched by things unseen. The forces would make the fire blaze up and then die down. Then you'd be shown transparent shadows, misty grey-looking entities. Gradually you would come to accept things of a different realm as part of the totality of reality and your fear of them would decrease. You come to accept that these things are always around us and understand that they are not evil."

Grandfather talked about being in a Navajo ceremony which sounded similar to my experience in Mountain Bear's Night Lodge ceremony. He said, "I saw blue flames appearing above me and felt wings brushing me and heard rattles going all around and up on the ceiling. Eventually, a rattle touched me in a very controlled manner, yet there was no person holding it. Accept these events as a gift. Don't think they are evil just because your mind cannot understand it," he emphasized.

As a young man, Grandfather said he heard and

saw a god in the desert. He went on to say, "It was something like a ringing in the ears, but it was all around my body. There were sparks and lights and a whirring sound. The god spoke to me, not through my ears, but to my thoughts. He gave me some instructions before leaving me."

As he grew older he would learn from four medicine men. One was Chumash, the others were Pueblo, Yaqui and Aztec, of the Toltec lineage. I recall Grandfather telling me "the Pueblo man I was learning from at the time was a huge, ugly guy with a big, crooked nose. Whenever we went to a new village for healings, the people were always scared when they first saw him. The children would run and hide." Grandfather continued, after chuckling, "But he was a very kind, gentle man and an effective healer."

"To become a healer part of my training was to experience visions which were prompted by ingesting sacred mushrooms. During one vision I woke up in a cave and one of the twin gods of my people appeared to me. I didn't know which one it was because they are identical. One is the god of the day, and the other is the god of the night. Being in a cave I couldn't tell if it was daytime or night. The god was several feet taller than me, with a muscular build and was shimmering like polished gold, radiating light throughout the cave. The god spoke to me and gave me my abilities, but also warned me of the challenges ahead in my life. The god gave me instructions and the awareness that specific information or knowledge would come to me as needed. I saw people on the 'other side' that I had known in life but wasn't aware that they had died. After four days and nights in the cave I returned to my people and was informed that those individuals had passed away during the time I was in the cave."

Grandfather was an apprentice for over thirty years. The final ceremony establishing him as a healer involved being branded on the inside of his left wrist with a piece of native copper about the size of a silver dollar.

Grandfather Semu, a renowned Chumash healer, spiritual guide, and seer. Grandfather was a cherished friend and teacher to the author. Photograph by Linda D. Archer, used by permission.

Chapter Eleven

Taking The Medicine

Shortly after one of my visits at Grandfather's place Mountain Bear came to me in a dream and directed me to hold a sweat lodge ceremony for the people at the ranch to experience. In the dream he reminded me of his belief: "These things are not just for Indian people." The dream had such clarity and force that I followed its directive, as Many Robes had advised to. With Tom's assistance, I helped construct a sweat lodge on the ranch and held a "non-Native" sweat. During the sweat I had an experience of traveling rapidly through space, reminiscent of my journey with Mountain Bear in the Night Lodge. Many of those who participated in the sweat lodge were very moved. Alexander, the owner of the ranch, became interested in having more such spiritual experiences. He asked me if it would be possible for Grandfather to lead some type of ceremony at the ranch. I think he hoped that Grandfather would bestow a blessing on the land and the activities there.

When I next saw Grandfather, I conveyed to him Alexander's request for a ceremony. He thought for a moment, then said, "I'll come to the ranch before winter and perform a very special ceremony for you and him." He didn't offer any details or specify what kind of ceremony it would be. Grandfather suggested that each us, alone, spend some time contemplating questions relating to our personal beliefs.

I felt the best way to contemplate these questions would be to fast in the mountains where I would not be distracted by the activities on the ranch. I drove up into the Coastal range and hiked up a mountain until I located an open, level area with a clear view over the ridges to the Pacific Ocean. From this spot I could look out over the dark blue ridges that flow from the mountain, forming deep valleys like giant furrows that dropped off to the coast. Beyond them the endless waters of the Pacific met the sky.

The weather was good so I was able to spend the next three days and nights there without a tent, sitting in the sun all day and lying under the stars at night. Although I took no food, I did have a canteen of water in case I got dehydrated from being exposed to the sun day in and day out. It was a little easier for me to do without food than it had been when I fasted on Mount Shasta, but thirst was more of a challenge because of the intense sunshine. Facing towards the east at daybreak, I could watch the sunrise until it was directly overhead, then I would turn to face west until the sun "sank" into the Pacific. After sunset I would lie down to gaze at the stars until drifting off to sleep.

I thought about the questions Grandfather had posed to us, including the concepts that had influenced and molded me. Just as we are all shaped by our childhood environment, my view of the world had been absorbed from my parents and from my Catholic upbringing. It occurred to me how deeply seated beliefs become in our psyche, becoming a part of who we are (our ego). And I became aware of how, once they are ingrained, we are willing to defend them at any cost. Some realizations came to me as to how certain beliefs I held were limiting me in what I felt I could achieve, while others were actually harmful to my self-image.

A deep sense of appreciation for my parents settled over me. I felt very fortunate to have had such kind, loving people in my life who always put the needs of others before themselves. Strong feelings of gratitude flooded through me for all the blessings in my life. I appreciated my good fortune to have had a loving family, good friends, and teachers. I reveled at all the beauty the earth held for us and was grateful for having eyes to see it.

While I was sitting in the sun on the second day a small bird that had been flitting around chirping in the trees swooped down and landed in a bush a few feet away. As I sat motionless, not giving it any attention, the little creature began to hop around chirping. It seemed that the bird was trying to get my attention or make me move, but I sat there like a stone. Failing to rouse me, it flew over and landed on my right shoulder where it could give me closer inspection. After chirping a few times the bird hopped closer to my ear, chirping louder, as if to be certain I was listening. To my amazement the little creature seemed content to rest there, chirping for several minutes before flying to a nearby bush to scold me. If it had some message for me, I was not able to translate it. I can't be certain it was the same bird, but the next day I had a similar visitor land and sit on my other shoulder, behaving in the same manner.

By the time I needed to return to the ranch I really didn't want to leave this mountain sanctuary. Maybe I hadn't resolved the underlying issues of my beliefs, but at least I'd achieved a deeper awareness of how they affected my thinking and behavior.

The day before the ceremony Grandfather returned to the ranch to give us more instructions. Although he still hadn't revealed what type of ceremony it would be, he suggested we eat nothing until after the event. As Grandfather, his nephew, Chamo, and I went for a walk around the property he suddenly announced to us that he was going to perform the "Shikiipish" (sacred mushroom) ceremony for Alexander and me. This announcement took Chamo and me by such surprise that Chamo's head snapped around with a shocked look on his face. His reaction gave me the feeling that this ceremony was quite out of the ordinary, especially for non-Natives to participate in.

Grandfather said, "Before beginning a sacred mushroom ceremony I send the medicine around the vicinity to protect the area. The medicine will cause anyone who shouldn't be here to leave. They themselves will decide to leave for some reason or other, without necessarily knowing why." Perhaps that was the purpose of our walk around the property, so that he could establish a protected zone.

Later that afternoon Grandfather met with Alexander and me privately and told us he was the last Chumash medicine man to hold the knowledge of this medicine (the sacred mushroom). He gave us our final instructions to prepare us for the experience.

"First you must ask yourself, am I ready for this medicine? Then ask yourself, Is the medicine ready for me? When you have ingested the medicine, do not act from your own thoughts. Only act when you hear a voice speaking to you. You are attempting to communicate with the fourth dimension, the Spirit World. It has to do with a way of life. Pay attention to who or what shows up. It might be a spirit helper. There is nothing terrifying about the medicine if you are in the proper frame of mind. The Spirit World is right here, all around us all the time. You will see that you knew a lot of things you didn't remember and you will learn about things inside you, things that were dormant within you until you took the medicine. You will never be the same. If you have illness within you the medicine can show you what is making you ill."

He said, "At a certain point during the night I become a prayer and something very extraordinary will occur. I will check on you immediately after the extraordinary event to be sure you are okay."

Just before dark, the three of us entered my cabin

where we would spend the next twelve hours. Grandfather smudged us with cleansing sage, and then he proceeded to smudge the whole cabin to purify the ceremonial setting. He instructed us to place our mattresses on the cabin floor, then he sang two songs before giving us each the appropriate amount of psycho-active mushrooms. According to him, the correct amount for each individual is the amount that fills the palm of their hand. Grandfather then stepped out of sight where he could focus and direct the event.

The dried mushrooms tasted earthy in my mouth, with a slightly inky flavor on the back of the tongue. As I lay down on my mattress I could sense the medicine moving through my bloodstream, similar to a mild electric current passing through my body. I shifted into an awareness that seemed to come from every cell in my body. There was no inclination to do anything other than lie on my back sensing the other energies in the room. There was a feeling of being disconnected from any normal sense of time. I did have a sense of being connected to all other living creatures by an invisible web.

Although I felt no physical discomfort and could move my body, I had little interest in doing anything other than observing the phenomena which were beginning to occur in the room. It seemed I was witnessing from a deeper part of myself than under normal conditions. I observed various forms made of light and lines of glowing light shimmering in the air around the room. These light patterns moved slowly through the air above us maintaining their form while moving about. Several of the lights were cane-shaped, while others were in grid-like patterns floating above us. My impression, or intuitive feeling, was that the light forms possessed awareness and hovered or moved about according to their own volition.

It occurred to me that these light forms were actually intelligent entities, but of a different nature than we humans. I wondered if they always inhabited our world, but were not visible to us under normal circumstances. Perhaps the sacred mushroom allowed for an expanded visual field to be available to us.

At some point in time I heard a soft whirring sound and noticed a luminous spinning disc, about two feet in diameter, slowly entering the cabin by passing through a closed window directly across from us. It brought to mind the notion of a hologram. The disc appeared to adjust its line of travel, curving slowly towards me, while it spun. Totally fascinated by this incredible sight, I lay on my back observing it as the disc came directly over my head and chest. It hovered and spun about two feet above me while emitting a barely audible humming sound or vibration. In complete awe and transfixed by it, my body became immobilized as I continued to stare at the disc. Its presence felt very benevolent. The disc rotated slowly enough to reveal an indiscernible pattern within or upon it.

After what seemed like several moments the luminous disc moved over to Alexander. As soon as I saw that it was spinning over him as it had over me, I averted my eyes so as not to intrude on his experience. Then it left in the same manner it had entered the cabin, through the closed window, never breaking it. I knew this phenomenon was of a different dimension, not a hallucination or an invention of our minds. Awestruck and speechless, we both lay there motionless and silent. There was no verbal communication between Alexander and me during the ceremony. However, I had an intuitive sense that we understood what the other was feeling and experiencing. I was absorbed in feelings of wonder and spiritual bliss.

Checking on us as he had promised, Grandfather appeared in the doorway with a big grin on his face. He asked in a gentle voice, "How are you doing?" I managed to say, "Wonderful, Grandfather," but that's all I could get out. I was still reveling in the astonishing experience. I looked over at Alexander who was smiling serenely, but remained silent. I never would have imagined such things existed or were possible to have personal experience of; I lacked words to express the incredible feelings of ecstasy and amazement. As Grandfather would later say, "There are no words for such things. They belong to another dimension."

Grandfather believed it is the experience itself_that held the importance of the event; to analyze these things somehow diminished them. His way was to contemplate the effect of the experience and aspects of what it revealed, without attempting any rational understanding. He said, "Just accept that you have been shown something and give thanks to the power that has revealed it to you. These things are gifts to us."

By daybreak the effect of the medicine was subsiding and my perceptions were returning to their normal state. Although we had been in the cabin all night it felt as if only a short time had passed.

This experience was as profound, although totally different, as the incredible ceremony Mountain Bear had performed. Both of those extraordinary men had spent many years of sacrifice, hardship and dedication to acquire spiritual helpers and to develop their abilities. Each of them, following their own unique path and culture, had achieved abilities that would be what most people would consider truly supernatural. Grandfather's ceremony was unique to him and perhaps he was the only living person who could bring these particular amazing realities through the veil of the fourth dimension so they could be witnessed by us.

Alexander and I briefly touched on and compared our experiences the following day, confirming we both witnessed the same phenomena. It is difficult to give these extraordinary events the description they deserve as supernatural phenomena. Perhaps there is no way to relate the full force of this event which defies rational understanding.

As a result of this profound experience I now had a greatly expanded concept of reality. Like Mountain Bear, Grandfather had again blown away the boundaries of what I had previously understood to exist and be possible. Furthermore, his ability to bring us the experience of the fourth dimension when and where he chose through his intention was far beyond what many of us who came into contact with him would understand him to be capable of. I had witnessed something few people would ever experience and I now knew his abilities were beyond anything I could have previously imagined. They were also beyond my rational grasp. As he had stated, "Reason is a valuable tool for mankind, but it can't explain the fourth dimension. There is more to the universe than reason."

I also knew our experience in the ceremony was beyond what anyone lacking that involvement would accept as believable. People who saw Grandfather simply as a charismatic old Indian lacked a true grasp of his depth and ability. But the awesome event deepened my respect and interest in this old man and his medicine ways. It would eventually lead me to a much deeper involvement with Grandfather and Native spiritual practices. It seemed I had been hooked by the Spirit World and could not put these experiences out of my mind.

Chapter Twelve

Learning from the Owl Man

I had been working at the ranch for a year and a half when Alex made the difficult decision to discontinue programs offered to the public. With his many business responsibilities in Germany the demands of the ranch required time and focus he felt he just couldn't give. He probably needed a break from the work and stress rather than more of the same. It wasn't long after the students, guests, and most of the staff had left that my feelings of loneliness began to settle in. Growing restless, I decided it was time to move on. I found employment at the Varian Arabian horse ranch roughly seventy miles closer to Grandfather's place.

Although I hadn't made a conscious decision to stop drinking alcohol, my interest and desire for alcoholic beverages had diminished since my time at Mountain Bear's. However, for whatever reason, one night in the summer of 83' I went to a tavern with a co-worker and drank three beers. The next evening I went to visit Grandfather on the mesa. I sat in a circle with eight or ten others, Native and non-native, listening to Grandfather as he told stories and answered our questions. Sitting directly across from Grandfather, I began to feel extreme discomfort in my belly area and had the sensation that an invisible hand was squeezing my intestines. I started sweating profusely. When I glanced over at Grandfather his face appeared to be very owl-like. It seemed as if he was concentrating or focusing on me.

I had a mental image of some invisible force coming from Grandfather's mid-section penetrating and wrenching my gut. The feeling was extremely uncomfortable and disconcerting. When the conversation ended and we left his cabin, Chamo advised me not to come around Grandfather if I had been using alcohol. He told me Grandfather could always tell who had been using alcohol recently and knew it was still in my system. The feeling I had experienced that evening was so unsettling that I didn't drink any alcohol for the next nine years while I was closely associated with Grandfather. I wanted to respect Grandfather's ways while in his presence and I never wanted to experience the discomfort I'd felt that night in his cabin.

As a consequence of the sacred mushroom ceremony and the experience of getting my guts wrenched that night on the mesa by some invisible force, I felt so intrigued that I yearned for a better grasp of this mysterious man's life. In addition to those events I had been having dreams in which Grandfather was showing me various aspects of the fourth dimension. My interest was to learn what I could about Grandfather's ways and incorporate them into my personal belief system. In early January of 1984 I left my job at the Arabian horse ranch and moved out to the mesa in order to fully immerse myself in his world.

I fixed up the loft in the little barn and installed a woodstove to make it comfortable for the winter. Grandfather arranged to have a woman living on the mesa cook for me, in exchange for keeping her and her young son supplied with firewood. I also looked after the goats, making certain they had fresh water and feed, and cared for the newborns. In addition to cutting firewood there were other chores and improvements to be made to the structures. Since there was no source of water on the mesa we would take Grandfather's pickup truck several miles up into the mountains and fill large water jugs at a mountain spring. This water would be used for drinking, cooking and watering the goats and chickens. Since all the water had to be hauled to the mesa, we would be very careful not to waste any. Water that had been used for cooking was later applied to the herb garden.

For washing and cleaning we would use alkali water from a nearby ranch in the valley below the mesa. I managed to shower using only one and one-half gallons of water, pouring it over me directly from a gallon jug. I'd start with a half gallon to soak down, then scrub with soap, and use the rest to rinse off. It was primitive, but effective.

I would spend some time with Grandfather most days. After dinner every evening I would go to his cabin to listen and ask questions. There he told stories intended to inform the listener about healing or other topics. I always looked forward to those evening sessions in his cabin. The setting on the isolated mesa, in the dark of night with the smell of sage wafting in the air, surrounded by medicine paraphernalia, in the company of this wise and unusual man, was especially magical.

He spoke about the early history of California and the destructive influence the Spanish Christian missions had on his people. Some of the stories were of his personal life, others concerned medicine men and women he knew. He imparted information about the preparation and usage of various herbs, and a range of other topics. Often there would be one or more people who were there for a few days for healings of ailments such as addictions, asthma, diabetes, nervous disorders and a range of other physical and emotional problems. Grandfather sometimes directed me to assist him in small ways during healing sessions.

During the years I was around him there were several veterans of the Vietnam War, both Native and non-Native, who came to him to get help with mental and emotional concerns as well as problems with alcohol. As I mentioned, Grandfather did not tolerate the use of alcohol. He said he had learned to drink when he was in the Navy and had his own bout with alcohol. He said every Indian is an alcoholic as soon as they begin to drink, since his people have no genetic immunity to it. He said, "First the man takes a drink, then the drink takes a drink, then the drink takes the man." He felt that most problem drinking was a way to escape guilt.

One evening Grandfather spoke about the world being destroyed before and said he was shown that at some time in the future not far off, "There would be little islands of people scattered around the earth." He warned that mankind has misused the gift of fire. He said that fire is an entity--it is our medicine. Like us, it burns oxygen and needs fuel. It can be suffocated and it can be drowned. Grandfather told us, "Fire was given to man for his protection to keep away ferocious animals, to give us light at night, to give us warmth and for preparing food. Man has made bigger and bigger fires to destroy each other. It can get out of control and destroy everything." He warned us against using fire for harm.

On another occasion Grandfather spoke about birds, which were very important to him. He explained, "The eagle is the ruler of the upper sky, the hawks rule the lower sky, and the owl is the ruler of the night sky and is also the messenger. Some Native Americans have a history of being afraid of the owl, thinking it forewarned something bad. The owl is just the messenger for good or bad."

"If you want to experience a transformation or shift in awareness, listen to the birds and observe what they do," Grandfather said.

He told me that one of his friends and teachers from Mexico, a Yaqui Indian, could transform himself into a crow. Grandfather told of being with this friend one day looking over some horses in a corral. Some Mexican Federalies showed up looking for the man. Grandfather said, "My friend went behind a large boulder in the corral, crouched down out of sight for a moment, and transformed himself into a crow. He then flew to a nearby tree and watched as the officials searched behind the boulder for him in dismay. When the officials left, the 'crow-man' flew down behind the boulder and then stepped out in his human form."

Grandfather never made any claims regarding his own abilities to transform himself, but I knew several people who believed he could shift into the bodily form of an owl. I had the impression he transformed himself into an owl that night at his cabin, when he wrenched my guts because I had been drinking the night before.

Returning to the mesa from the village one afternoon, I found in the road the corpse of a small owl that must have been recently hit by a vehicle. Knowing Grandfather was of the Owl Clan, and curious as to how best to preserve the little creature, I asked Grandfather for his advice. He told me how to prepare the skull and preserve the wings and feathers. After cleaning the owl skull and burying it in sand to allow the little bugs to finish cleaning it, I tacked the separated wings on the wall over my bed as he'd advised.

During the night I had the experience of the owl wings coming off the wall behind me and attaching themselves to my left and right temples. I felt fully awake. Then the wings began to move and I was lifted in a prone position up towards the ceiling. When my body was four or five feet above the bed and getting close to the ceiling I panicked, thinking I was going to smash into it. That thought brought me crashing like a rock back onto the bed. Covered in a cold sweat, I heard myself involuntarily call out for Grandfather.

When I awoke in the morning I was amazed to find the wings lying on my pillow next to my head. When I saw Grandfather later that morning he was grinning as he asked how I had slept. When I told him what had occurred during the night he said, "That was a good beginning, but try just going with it the next time. Put your fear aside and trust in the journey." The following night I dreamt the wings were lifting me towards the ceiling again. This time I allowed them to carry me out into the night sky, where I glided effortlessly above the desert, soaring through the night like an owl observing the surroundings. The sensation of gliding through the night sky was thrilling and left me feeling ecstatic when I awoke.

After I'd related some of my recent dreams with Grandfather, he told me he believed I had an aptitude for dreaming. Grandfather said, "My people believed in the power of dreams and visions. They made a tea from herbs to encourage clear dreaming."

He also told me his people used a small steatite pipe from which they smoked what he called coyote tobacco, also known as desert tobacco, to help them experience meaningful visions. He then went into his bedroom, returning with a dark green, solid stone pipe about eight inches long. "This is one of those pipes. It's very old." Grandfather stated that "dreams are often symbolic, but visions are real. Don't analyze them. Just accept them. During some visions an animal might come to help you and speak to you. It might tell you to kill it and to use its hide for your medicine bundle. That's the only time it's okay to kill something other than for food. Visions are real. Once you touch this power you will be a different person. Accept the power or experience. When something unusual happens, give a welcome to things of the other worlds. It is our thoughts that make them dissolve. Your eyes do not see what is not there. They don't play tricks on us. It's the mind that plays tricks."

One morning Grandfather and I went out to hunt rabbits for a meal he liked to prepare with roasted cactus. The barrel of his old single shot .22 caliber rifle was taped to the gun stock with electrical tape, which made me question its accuracy. As we moved through the scrub brush, rabbits would burst out of the brush, zigzagging away. I never understood why Grandfather was always in a good shooting position in relation to the rabbits, while I was not. He would whistle sharply, causing the rabbit to pause for a second, while he quickly raised his rifle and, without hesitating, fire a shot hitting the rabbit in the head. Although he seemed not to aim, his bullet always found its mark. He said, "You have to shoot them in the head so they die instantly and don't suffer. That would ruin the meat."

During the nine months I stayed with Grandfather on the mesa there were several occasions when rattlesnakes were too close for comfort. One evening we were eating dinner in Grandfather's cabin when a large rattler crawled in from under the cabin wall. When I offered to kill it Grandfather scolded me. In a stern voice he said, "They have a right to be here on the land also. They belong to the earth and have a right to life just as we do." He then taught me how to catch it using a broom handle with a clothes line rope tied at the handle end with a loop in it. I carefully placed the loop end of the rope over the snake's head while standing off to the side, allowing the loop to go around the base of the snake's head. Then I quickly tightened the rope from the other end so that it was snug around the rattler's neck. With the rope tight around the snake, I lifted it into a garbage can and placed the lid on just as I loosened the rope and pulled the broom handle away. I put the garbage can in my jeep and took it further out into the desert and released the snake.

On several occasions I found rattlers resting next to the goat water trough. During that summer I caught and released six rattlers using this method. When I laid the garbage can on the ground and knocked the lid off to let them go, some would rattle loudly before crawling away. I wondered if they were thanking me for sparing their life and freedom, or just pissed about the forced move.

While living on the mesa I would drive for Grandfather when he was traveling to speak at various gatherings in Ojai or Ventura, California. After a talk Grandfather gave in Ventura one night, we stopped for a snack before making the drive home. Although he seldom ate sweets, he ordered chocolate cake that night. The waitress brought him a very large piece. As we were going up Ventura canyon I noticed a strong odor in his Toyota pickup and realized the old Indian was passing gas. He had little tolerance for sugar and even with the windows down we were all gagging for air. I pulled over next to the cliff so we could get out and let the truck air out. Grandfather went to the edge of the cliff and squatted down to relieve himself. He was dangerously close to the edge, so Eneke Alish and I each grabbed one of his arms so he wouldn't tip over backwards and tumble down the cliff. The old man was still passing gas and we were laughing so hard we almost lost our grip on him. There was thunder in the canyon that night and we laughed all the way home.

Chapter Thirteen

What the Ancients Knew

The information that follows was shared by Grandfather in bits and pieces during the many evenings I spent in his company over the years. Typically, one question was all it took to lead to an extended discourse on his part. We were talking about various religious beliefs one evening when I asked, "Grandfather, at what point in time does the soul join the body? At the time of conception?"

He said, "I believe that our spirit or soul enters our body with our first breath and leaves with our last exhale."

He went on to say, "Everyone has their own way of religion. It is different for desert people, forest people and seashore people. The way of the land is the religion. All our teachings are the laws of nature, and nature is god. Our gods walked with us on this land and gave us instructions on how to live. All the gods exist, but are only active when people pray to them; otherwise, they are dormant. For example, when you hear a bird singing in the morning you are hearing a prayer from nature. Be thankful for that and bring the gods alive. Be thankful also that you are a part of the creation and can hear its song. We cannot grasp the whole of creation. Each of us can understand only a part of it. That's why I think of it as 'the Great Mystery.' There is power in everything, every animal, if one knows how to use it. There is power in an eagle feather."

Grandfather was speaking at a gathering when he was asked how one can receive a medicine pouch. A medicine pouch is a small prayer bundle that hangs around the neck and protects the wearer from negative forces. Grandfather said, "They are only given to those who go through a special ceremony and who are considered one of our own. In other words, you need to be Native American or be adopted by Native Americans to receive one. I think the most important aspect is the thought or prayer put into the pouch. That is what gives it its potency."

He always stressed how important and powerful our thoughts are. "Good thoughts towards another are like a prayer for them (good medicine). Negative thoughts towards another can actually cause harm to the other and to yourself. Always be grateful for what you have and don't envy others. Pray only for health and happiness. My people didn't pray for money because they didn't know what it would bring with it."

Grandfather was always very inclusive towards non-Native people and I always felt he treated everyone respectfully, no matter what their background or beliefs. But by now I had come to realize that there is substantial controversy among Indigenous people as to what is and what is not appropriate to share with non-Natives. While we sat around a fire one evening I asked Grandfather to share his thoughts about non-Indians taking up Native practices.

"Grandfather, some Native people resent non-Natives being involved with and adopting their spiritual practices. Do you think these ways should be shared with the world or kept within the Native cultures?"

He replied, "You don't have to be Indian to utilize Native American sacred practices, but your mind needs to be in the right place. All things now should be available to anyone with a good heart, but you need to be sincere. Seeking spiritual phenomena has no rules. Each of us is psychic. It is the beginning of understanding. This is the 1980's and a new people are coming into being who recognize the need to utilize knowledge from a variety of cultures. Today there are healers of various mixes of race and culture utilizing techniques adopted from diverse traditions. The clock cannot be turned back and everyone should have access to the truth. It is the set of your heart, your intention, that determines your path. Find your own path, incorporating what is true, while being respectful of others' ways. People who take up these ways have to have a good heart and not try to be something they are not. If you misuse these things you will have problems in your life. The law of retribution states: 'You will lose that which you love the most.' Problems can occur in your family for several generations. Remember that everyone is different. Live your own path."

Grandfather told me that the Druids had a world view and spiritual practice that was essentially the same as that of North American Indians, and that those descended from the Celts could learn much from the ways of their own ancestors, who also had a nature-based religion.

"Your ancestors held deep understandings of the laws of nature, but much of their knowledge has been forgotten over the generations. This is the time for that knowledge to be re-discovered and put into practice."

"Everyone's path is different, but they all meet at the top of the mountain. When we die we go into another dimension, but we are still here as part of the universe. Death does not discriminate; it takes everyone. I think we all end up in the same place." he said.

One evening during a discussion about how our behavior is controlled by our thoughts Grandfather made the following statements regarding the subconscious mind. He said, "The sub-conscious is fully formed by the time we are born and it is receptive to outside influences. Suggestions were made to the subconscious mind of infants to affect their future behavior. For example, you will be a good boy or girl so that by the time the conscious mind is developed you will already know how to behave and know right from wrong. Behavior is born in the subconscious. It is the inner workshop of the mind and we need to learn to control our minds."

Grandfather said many physical problems begin with how we think about ourselves or by guilt imposed upon us by our beliefs or the influence of the church. "Disease starts outside you and attaches itself to your body," he said. "It can grow and get into your body. In order to master our subconscious we need to give it positive input and practice feeling good about ourselves." He continued, saying, "Don't be involved in gossip or in holding negative thoughts towards others. That will harm only you. Participating in denigrating conversations or demeaning thoughts of others attracts negativity to our minds."

"How does the concept of sin effect our mental attitudes?", I asked.

"Prior to the coming of Christianity to our land, Indians didn't believe in or know about sin," he stated. "There was only crime; do wrong and you would be punished or exiled. Churches use guilt, sins, and fear to control people. These are very damaging forces to our subconscious minds and result in problems later in life. If we carry guilt about the past we need to drop the guilt. Guilt often causes people to turn to alcohol. The past is gone. Its over. Leave the guilt behind. It serves no positive purpose but can continue to harm us psychically and physically. Everything starts in the mind. If you think about something, it will often happen. Concentrate on it and it can become reality. If we believe we have sinned, we feel guilty, and believe we should be punished. So we punish ourselves. People often bring illness upon themselves in order to punish themselves. We must accept ourselves, including our bodies."

The only time I ever heard Grandfather swear

during all the years I was around him was when I asked him what he thought about the concept of original sin. "That's bullshit!", he said. "Children are born innocent. Children are not born with sin or prejudices. They learn these things from their parents and society."

I recalled Rolling Thunder having said, "If you don't know right from wrong you are innocent, but once you know the difference you are then responsible for your actions."

Our conversation apparently stirred his memory as he said, "There are certain influences on us that can be passed down through the generations, although they are different from the concept of original sin." Even though the physical umbilical cord connecting us to our mother is cut when we are born, Grandfather believed that there is an invisible genetic umbilical cord which keeps us connected to thought patterns and behavior that belonged to our forbearers. We are thus under the influence of our ancestors. Negative behavior or psychological problems could be passed down to us through the generations. According to him, "The genetic cord cutting ceremony only eliminates negative ancestral influences. Positive influences are not affected because whatever is positive is true, and truth cannot be destroyed."

Several weeks later he conducted the genetic cord-cutting ceremony on me. He used a razor-sharp obsidian knife with an eight-inch blade, while Eneke Alish sang the accompanying songs. At a given time, he made a quick slice with the knife to sever the genetic cord. Grandfather said, "Cutting the genetic umbilical cord removes the pull of the past. Now you are responsible for your thoughts and actions. You now have free will."

Four months after I moved to the mesa Grandfather asked me to take Karin, a woman who also lived there, to New Mexico so she could be treated by a Navajo medicine man he knew. Karin had been suffering from intense anxiety and severe headaches. She believed she was a victim of a psychic attack by someone involved in witchcraft. Grandfather felt the Navajo healer, Tewa, had expertise in this realm and could help her. Having heard the practice of witchcraft was common in the southwest, I questioned Grandfather about my own safety in making this journey. "You are protected," he said, in a reassuring tone of voice. I had long been skeptical of the reality of witchcraft. I wondered if I was protected because of my lack of belief. On the other hand, I was convinced about Grandfather's extraordinary abilities and knowledge regarding the occult. I also thought that his wrenching my guts that evening in his cabin could be a form of witchcraft, although the effects were ultimately positive. Alcohol would never again be a problem for me.

Wanting a better understanding of the practice of witchcraft, I asked why people became involved with such practices. He told me, "Some enter the dark side for purposes of revenge or jealousy or envy. A witch or practitioner of the dark side will look for an opening in you and penetrate that point. One needs to fill in the gaps or holes in oneself in order to be protected, as you have now done. A real witch always leaves an opening when they send a negative charge. That way a knowledgeable person can block or defuse the situation. Amateur witches don't do this or don't know how to do this. Therefore they are the most dangerous. However, there are ways to turn things around and send the charge back to them. They will then suffer the consequences of their actions." Grandfather proceeded to tell me about his own experiences of helping people who had been victims of witchcraft and his techniques for returning the "charge" to its originator.

Grandfather made all the necessary preparations, setting up Karin's meeting with Tewa, acquiring a relatively new, fuel-efficient vehicle for the trip, and arranging for places for me to stay while in New Mexico. The drive was long and stressful not so much because of the distance, but because of the tension in the car due to Karin's anxiety and her lack of acceptance of me. Being trapped in the car together for hours was a challenge for both of us. It made me wonder if Grandfather was testing my patience. I imagined him having a good laugh over the thought of Karin and I locked in the same car for hours on end.

After many hours on the road we arrived in New Mexico and located Tewa's home where she was to be treated. She later told me several objects that appeared to be tiny pins and bones were drawn out of her forehead with the use of crystals. The Navajo healer then recommended that she spend a few days in the care of a Native woman who incorporated Christian prayers in her healing practice. Karin was surprised and disappointed that the old medicine man had recommended she visit a Christian healer. She was at first distrustful and dubious about being treated by a Christian, but finally relented in hope of getting relief from her anxiety.

Since Karin's healing would require being in that area several days, Grandfather had arranged for me to stay with a traditional Navajo family during that time. My first night there I was awakened by loud barking and fierce scratching sounds on the door and walls of their home. I knew they didn't have a dog. The ferocity of the scratching and growling seemed more aggressive than what a dog would be capable of. Whatever it was seemed very determined to force its way into the home. Everyone in the house remained quiet and no one got up to investigate, so I was reluctant to go out to check things out.

The next day I was informed by the family that the noises I had heard were made by a "skin walker". They explained that a "skin walker" was a person who is following the dark path and through morbid rituals can transform themselves into something like a large coyote. This seemed to be a common occurrence for them and they regularly performed rituals to protect themselves.

The following afternoon an elderly medicine woman came to visit. Her hair was white but her complexion and figure were that of a very young woman. She was incredibly beautiful, dressed in traditional Navajo style, and emanated holiness and serenity. I felt that I was in the presence of a saint. Never having seen a woman of her age with such beautiful skin and features, I marveled at her radiance. Her calming presence and prayers dispelled the negativity of the previous night.

Two days later I visited another Navajo family living in a traditional hogan in the desert south of Farmington. When I questioned why they had a padlock on their outhouse they informed me they had been attacked by witchcraft in the past and were concerned someone might put something with a negative charge in the outhouse. They also brought in all their clothes from the clothesline before dark to prevent the theft of one of their garments, which might then be used against them.

Four days after arriving in New Mexico, I picked Karin up at the home of the Christian healer. She was noticeably calmer and more pleasant. She acknowledged her time with the Christian healer had been very helpful. Although she held no affection for me, she was actually smiling and joking with me now, which made the trip home much more relaxed and enjoyable. From my observations the effects of her healing endured for at least the next five months, after which I never saw her. Upon our return I was extremely fortunate to get a seasonal job with the Cuyama Recreation Department, since it was the only employment available for over 100 miles.

As he grew older, Grandfather often expressed a concern that there was no one who would carry on his knowledge. I felt I could apply what Grandfather had taught me to my own life and I knew I could relate some of that information to others, but felt it was not appropriate for me to pursue a role which properly belonged to an indigenous person. In the years to come, I would witness some of the difficulties other non-Native people encountered when they took on responsibilities and positions traditionally held by Native spiritual leaders.

Knowing that the information and experiences that had been shared with me should not be lost forever with the passing of this elder, I tried to retain as much as possible from the many evenings spent with Grandfather. I made some notes for future reference to preserve some of these teachings for whomever might find some value or insights from them. This initiated my first thoughts about recording Grandfather's wisdom. Each person who spent much time around Grandfather had picked up various aspects of his knowledge. Perhaps those pieces of information would be brought together someday into a more comprehensive unit and carried forth by the right person.

As fall was approaching, my job with the Parks Department was coming to an end. Once again I was feeling what Grandfather called the wanderlust. I had been with Grandfather on a daily basis for the past nine months and was ready for a break from the demands of being in an intense state of awareness. Also, I was lonesome for more frequent female companionship and the camaraderie of people my age. Although I'd become attached to Grandfather, it was time to focus on my own needs. In early October, 1984, I told him I was ready to set off for a new adventure.

Chapter Fourteen

Breitenbush and Tribal Life

I drove to Northern California to visit Connie, a friend who was a resident employee at Harbin Hot Springs north of San Francisco. I'd spent a couple days relaxing and soaking in the mineral springs before meeting Jes and Gaia, who were preparing to travel to Breitenbush Hot Springs, a retreat/conference center in the Cascade mountains of Oregon. I decided to caravan to Oregon with them and their two young sons to investigate possible job opportunities. The facility was operated as a cooperative, intentional community of approximately thirty residents and a dozen part-time helpers. All were dedicated to preserving the many natural hot springs and hosting conferences relating to a variety of meditation, personal growth, and spiritual development programs.

The Breitenbush River runs through the center of the property, separating the conference/retreat center from the resident community. Forty guest cabins and a large old rustic lodge, where conferences are held and meals served, are located on one side of the river. Houses and cabins for the staff and permanent residents are on the opposite side of the river. Part of the attraction for the guests are the many hot mineral springs, the rustic steam sauna and the surrounding old-growth forest.

All power and heat are produced on site directly from the natural resources on the property. Water diverted from the river is channeled through a sluice way to a turbine at the edge of the river, providing electricity for the retreat center, cabins and houses. A closed system of piping carries cold river water deep below the surface through hot geothermal bedrock. The heat in the earth is transferred through the pipes, warming the water in the pipes and causing the heated water to rise to surface. The water is then pumped to all the buildings to provide heat.

I was immediately taken with the natural beauty of the property and surrounding mountain forests. I was also impressed with the dedication of the residents toward preserving the grounds and their commitment to community ideals. Breitenbush held opportunities for the social life I'd put aside while living on the mesa with Grandfather. Social gatherings involving community members and guests centered around music, dance, and ceremony. It felt as if we were a tribe of sorts, focused on environmental consciousness and personal growth. It was the ideal situation at this point in my life, with a constant flow of guests and interesting conferences, which residents could attend for free or at reduced charge.

For the next three years I lived in a small cabin near the bank of the river, at the northern edge of the community, surrounded by old-growth forest. Initially I assisted with carpentry and maintenance projects. Then I took a position in the office, helping to arrange conferences.

Breitenbush offered a variety of meditation and personal growth retreats. However, there were none that focused on indigenous practices lead by actual Native Americans. I began to reach out to traditional Native people from Oregon and was eventually put in touch with Al Smith, a respected Klamath elder. With Al's cooperation I organized a three-day event in the spring of 1985 featuring a number of Native speakers and workshop leaders. We constructed a sweat lodge on the bank of the Breitenbush River where Al led the first of the many sweat lodge ceremonies over the next few years.

Sometimes as many as four sweat lodge ceremonies would be held during one weekend. We would often have a sweat lodge on Friday evening, another at sunrise on Saturday morning, one that evening, and one more at sunrise on Sunday.

Early in my first summer there I traveled to the Warm Springs reservation, a four-hour drive from Breitenbush, to inquire if there were any elders there who might have used the hot springs prior to its development in the early 1920's. After a brief meeting with members of the counsel of the Bureau of Indian Affairs and getting no leads, I began randomly stopping at homes on the reservation to ask about elders. I was invited into one home at which the family was very friendly. But they told me they were "beer-drinking Indians" and didn't participate in traditional ways. They did, however, direct me to the home of Andrew David, a medicine man in his mid-nineties.

When I drove up towards his home I was met by his son-in-law, who was on horseback, moving some cattle towards a corral across from the house. I inquired for Andrew and was told to go on in the house and see if he was awake. "If he's in his rocking chair he'll be up for company," his son-in-law told me. Andrew was sitting in his rocking chair near the back wall of his house. He was a lean man with long white braids hanging down to his belt. He wore a baseball cap with fancy beading in the brim. The old man was very friendly and seemed pleased to have someone there interested in what he might have to say.

After introducing myself I inquired if he, or anyone he knew, had ever been at Breitenbush. Seemingly ignoring my question, he said, "My religion is called 'The Way of the Three Feathers' and the first premise of my religion is to respect all other faiths." Andrew then went on talking about his life and beliefs for an hour or more. Eventually he said he didn't know anyone who had visited the hot springs I was referring to. He did tell me about an elderly woman living near Simnasho, in the northern part of the reservation, who might have some knowledge of what I was curious about.

I spent the night in my tent and continued my search for the woman the next day. When I arrived at the area I'd been directed to I stopped at another house to inquire for her. It turned out to be the home of an old Indian bronc rider whose daughters had made a display of his many awards and trophies that he'd won in rodeos over the years. The old guy and his daughters were very friendly and engaging. He showed me an exercise he used prior to mounting rodeo broncs. He began by first lifting one fist to his forehead and bringing it down to the opposite raised knee, and then repeating this with the other fist and opposite knee. He said he would repeat this movement for several minutes before climbing on a bronc. He told me, "This will give you better balance and your body will adjust quicker to the horse's movements." I didn't ask him where he had learned that, but it struck me as something that was valid. He said he didn't know about the hot springs I was asking about, but said the woman I was looking for lived in the next house further down the road. As I walked out the door he said, "You know you can remember everything. There is a way to train your mind to do that."

Sylvia welcomed me into her home and we had a warm visit. She was one of three sisters who were respected carriers of the traditions and a descendent of a sister of Chief Joseph of the Nez Perce. She told me she remembered stopping to rest and soaking in the pools of Breitenbush valley as a young girl when her people were moving from their winter camp west of the Cascades to their summer place at Warm Springs. Sylvia invited me to come back again to meet her sons, Jim and Milt.

Two weeks later I returned with a friend, Michael Donnelly. Her son Jim took us out to Milt's place. Milt was in his mid-thirties and had been raised by a traditional elder in the old ways. He was well known in the northwest as a singer, drummer and sun dancer. We had similar social and political views and eventually developed a lasting connection. We made excursions into the mountains and caves and I later traveled with him and others to the Southwest and Mexico.

Upon our return I invited the group to Breitenbush. Three of the grandmothers from Warm Springs came with the group and prepared a traditional salmon feast over an open fire. These elder women were held in high regard by the Native people in that region as keepers of the traditions. Their authority was never questioned or challenged by the younger people. As our friendship developed, they invited several of us to the Sacred Sundance, a multi-tribal event held near Mount Hood, Oregon, each summer. Over the years there had been a migration of people escaping the depressing conditions on reservations in the Dakotas. Many of them had jumped on a train and ridden it as far west as they could. Ending up in Portland, Oregon, they organized the Sundance near Mt. Hood.

I spent a week at the Sundance grounds that summer assisting with security. I fasted for four days, along with many others, as a way of lending support to the sun dancers. The Sundance leader, Brave Buffalo, an Ogallala Sioux, stood about 6'6", with a broad chest and wide face. I had met him the previous summer when Grandfather Semu introduced me to him at a spiritual gathering in central California. Wearing a buffalo cape and headdress, Brave Buffalo led the sun dancers into the sacred circle where they were to endure the heat and sun for four days without food or water while they danced around the sacred tree.

The Sacred Sundance is an awesome and powerful event. Just being a witness and supporter at the Sacred Sundance was a transformative experience. What follows is a very brief description of this special ceremony. Only Native people who are involved in this unique rite can give one a deeper understanding of the Sacred Sundance. The participants prepare by being counseled by the spiritual leader, cleansing in sweat lodges and fasting. At some point their flesh is pierced with buffalo bones attached to a leather rope, which is tied to the sacred tree in the center of the arbor. Some drag buffalo skulls connected to ropes attached to buffalo bones which have been pierced into their upper backs, others hang from the sacred tree. Eventually they break free of the thong to offer their flesh to the creator for the healing of all peoples and the Earth. They dance so the people may continue to live.

Another reason the men go through this ritual is so they can feel compassion for the pain and suffering that women go through during childbirth. Nowadays, after World War II, women also participate in the Sundance, although they do not pierce their flesh, since they give their blood to the Earth when menstruating.

There were many sweat lodge ceremonies led by a number of elders at the Sundance. During one of those ceremonies in which all the warriors had entered the lodge with their hair braided, the elder told them the braid represented the unity of mind, body, and spirit. He then told them that he didn't wear his hair braided because he didn't have it all together yet. In other words, he wasn't evolved enough to wear his hair in braids. The deep respect the warriors held for this elder, combined with the feeling they were not as evolved as him, resulted in all of them immediately unbraiding their hair in the lodge. This explanation of the braid gave me another small insight into the depth and symbology of Native traditions.

Due to our connections with Native people, Jes, Gaia, and I became their main intermediaries at Breitenbush. Through our invitation many sun dancers and sacred pipe carriers came to Breitenbush to lead sweat lodge ceremonies. Spiritual leaders including Wallace Black Elk, Brave Buffalo, Martin High Bear, and Grandfather Semu, led a variety of ceremonies. We also hosted Native American political action groups for conferences and personal healings.

A number of challenging issues arose from the interaction of the Native people with members of the Breitenbush community. Because only vegetarian cuisine was served or allowed, community members became disgruntled when some Native people brought meat or fish for their meals. Other culture clashes developed concerning smoking in non-approved areas and bringing dogs to the property.

The policy was that only seeing-eye dogs were allowed. As their hosts, it was up to Jes, Gaia and me to work through these issues with the Breitenbush community and our Native guests, who were unaccustomed to these rules. Community members were reluctant to make exceptions, feeling Native people needed to abide by guidelines that had been established for good reason, while Native people resisted yielding to the policies imposed upon them by the community. These disparate views created stress for those of us who hosted the gatherings, but over time both groups became more accepting of each other's position and the tensions decreased dramatically.

Another group of Native men came to Breitenbush that summer. Among them was a master totem carver, Paul Red Cloud from Montana. We decided to make use of a large fir tree that had fallen into the river upstream from the sweat lodge. A group of us cut the tree and floated it downstream a few hundred feet to a spot where we could pull it up onto the river bank. With assistance from Jim Robideau from South Dakota and Mike Berry of the Warm Springs Reservation, Paul carved a magnificent totem pole from the fallen tree. This totem pole represents images of endangered wildlife species. Upon its completion a large group of us carried it from the river bank up the hill to a place near the center of the conference area where it was erected. Mike Berry offered prayers to consecrate the totem pole.

My days off from work at Breitenbush were spent hiking or cross-country skiing in the old-growth forest of the surrounding mountains by myself or with one or more others. Michael Donnelly, an avid outdoorsman and environmentalist, took me deep into the wilderness to a huge cave situated in a rock face, near the summit of a bald, rocky peak.

The cave can only be reached by traversing a long mountainous trail to the rocky peak, then along a narrow trail in the rock shelf on the eastern face of the mountain. This side of the peak drops straight off to the valley below. It's the kind of place where one misstep could be disastrous. The effort required is worth it, though, as the place is awe-inspiring. The opening to the cave is a fifty-foot high, wide arch with a deep valley below. Partially eroded grottos near the face of the cave contain natural rock sculptures reminiscent of statues of saints.

The inside of the cathedral-shaped cave is very roomy, reaching back well over sixty feet to a flat wall, where water seeps onto the floor of the cave, forming a small pool in a rock basin fifteen feet from the rear wall. Small green plants struggle towards the rays of sunlight which enter the mouth of the cave for an hour or two in the morning.

Over the next two years I made several visits to this powerful womb in the earth, spending nights in the cave by myself, or sometimes with others. On a short vision quest there by myself in the silence of the night, all I could hear was the sound of water dripping from the rock wall at the back of the cave. With no fire there was total darkness within this chamber of rock, but a portion of the sky was visible through the entrance. It was an excellent place for contemplation, especially when the weather was not conducive to being outside. It always felt nurturing to be so deep inside this mountain of rock, sheltered and isolated from the rest of the world. I guided a small group of Native people to this special place where they held a night-long Peyote meeting.

Of the many conference leaders who came to Breitenbush, I was most impressed with Ram Dass. While working at the registration desk, checking people in, I glanced up to see him patiently standing in the long line. Typically conference leaders expected special treatment, never waiting in a line, except perhaps at mealtime. On another occasion I was washing dishes in the back room of the dining hall. Ram Dass suddenly popped in and offered to help. Reluctantly, I put him to work. He said something to the effect, "We all seek enlightenment, but someone still needs to do the dishes."

Chapter Fifteen

Touching the Buffalo Heart

The following summer I attended another Sundance ceremony near Mount Hood lead by Brave Buffalo. A friend had invited me to his wedding in northern California scheduled for the Saturday after the Sundance. I had been told Brave Buffalo would be officiating the marriage ceremony, but with all the activity and concentration on the Sundance the wedding had temporarily slipped my mind. After the Sundance ended, I returned to Breitenbush for a couple of days and then packed my backpack, planning to hitchhike the several hundred miles to the wedding, which was to be held in a remote location. Earlier that summer I had given my Jeep to a family from the Warm Springs Reservation. They had a young boy and infant daughter, and were in greater need of a vehicle than I was.

Heidi, a friend from Breitenbush, asked if she could hitchhike with me, since she was headed in the same direction, trying to get to another location further south in California. We were picked up by a Native American alcohol and drug counselor, who got us down out of the mountains and dropped us off at the main highway. Heidi was interested in Native American spirituality and, being aware of my involvement with indigenous people, thought it was some kind of a "sign" that we had been given a ride by a Native person. I took it to be simply happenstance, but it reminded me that Brave Buffalo was to be officiating the wedding, and I figured he would take one of the two main roads from the Sundance grounds to northern California. I started visualizing his van coming down the road towards us.

It all seemed very far-fetched to think that we might catch a ride with him. After all, maybe he had already passed by here or taken a different route. I didn't mention anything about these thoughts to Heidi, as it seemed too improbable. After hitchhiking for an hour and a half without any luck, we climbed a small hill to get some shade and rest. When we went back to the highway and still had no luck getting a ride, I started concentrating on Brave Buffalo in his painted van. Moments later I saw his van coming over the hill and it was in the right lane closest to where we were standing.

I hollered "Brave Buffalo," as he sailed past us. Fortunately, Robert, his assistant, was sitting in the passenger seat with the window partly down, and heard me holler. Brave Buffalo pulled over and we climbed in the van.

"Where are you headed"? Brave Buffalo asked. "I'm headed for the wedding near Susanville that you are officiating, Heidi is going further south," I replied. But Heidi was so amazed at the coincidence she changed her plans and decided to travel on to the wedding with us.

I wondered what the odds were of this happening. The timing was perfect, as we had just come down from the hill and resumed hitchhiking just before the van appeared. Brave Buffalo had to be in the right lane of traffic, and his helper had to hear me holler. Furthermore, the wedding was several hundred miles away and off the beaten track. I was now assured of making it to my friend's wedding on time. With all the variables it did seem more than mere coincidence that we connected with him.

The night prior to the wedding Brave Buffalo led a sweat lodge ceremony. Before beginning the ceremony he passed sticks of sage around, advising us to place them behind our ears. He said, "They are like antennas that are tuned to the Spirit World." After the sweat lodge I went to a nearby stream to rinse off and recover from the intense heat. As I was sitting on the rocks at the edge of the stream, Brave Buffalo came and sat across the stream facing me. His mood was somber, and I sensed that he wasn't feeling his best. He told me, "There might be situations in the future when you will need to lead sweat lodges to help people get through hard times. There may not be Native Americans available to lead the sweat lodge and you will have to take on that responsibility." He was referring to the coming time of earth changes when people would need these ways to help them through.

I was surprised by his statement because I knew that some Native Americans felt it was not appropriate for a non-Native to lead sweat lodges. Besides, I felt the weight of the responsibility to conduct myself and the ceremony properly. He said something to the effect that, "We need to get beyond prejudice and recognize we all share this life and this planet. Healing ourselves and Mother Earth should be our priority." We waited by the stream until we had recovered enough to make our way back to the area where we were all camped. I invited him to come to Breitenbush to speak and lead a sweat lodge ceremony, which he did later that year.

It was a cloudless day, the temperature in the mid-nineties, with no breeze. After we completed setting-up the wedding arbor some of us sought out shade under the trees to get a reprieve from the heat. Brave Buffalo came over and scolded us for hiding from the sun. "Get out here in the sunlight," he said. "The sun will make you stronger."

Several of us had attended the Sundance the previous week, supporting the dancers as they endured the intense sun and heat. Now we had been reprimanded by the Sundance leader for being weak. We all readily obeyed his command and made sure we weren't caught lingering in the shade again.

When the big drum was set up and the singers and drummers were ready, Brave Buffalo proceeded to unite the bride and groom in a very heartfelt, personalized wedding ceremony. After the feast we sang and danced late into the night to the heartbeat rhythm of the drum. Attending the wedding ceremony ignited Heidi's fascination with Native traditions and she became a very dedicated supporter of indigenous practices.

Two months later Brave Buffalo came to Breitenbush as he had promised. During a conversation with a group of vegetarians, he was asked why it was necessary to eat meat. Brave Buffalo explained, "The buffalo is the greatest vegetarian of all. He eats the grasses and turns them into concentrated protein for us to eat, so we don't have to spend all day grazing. Mother Earth works twenty-four hours a day to provide us with food and shelter." Later during the sweat lodge he shared these words: "If you are sincere in your efforts to make changes in your life, the spirits will meet you half way. The spirit world is ready to assist us if we make a genuine attempt to change our ways." He also said, "When a person has led a good life the Creator will have prepared a lodge for him. The lodge will be filled with all that one has given away in his or her life, including kindness, love, and compassion."

Chapter Sixteen

Experiencing Deeper Seeing

In the summer of 1986 I was invited to attend a Native American Church meeting in northern California. Ingesting peyote cactus is central to this ceremony and I had wanted to experience this sacrament under the proper conditions for some time. The purpose of the meeting was to pray for the healing of a ten-year-old boy with severe vision problems. After modern medicine had not been successful in improving his vision, the boy's mother had requested and sponsored the meeting as a last hope. A secondary purpose for the meeting was to pray for the Native people of the Big Mountain area in Arizona who were being relocated from their ancestral lands by the U.S. Government so it could sell the mineral rights.

Several of us spent most of the day erecting a large teepee and making the crescent-moon altar for the Grandfather Peyote inside the teepee. Just after sunset we entered the teepee and took our places around the perimeter. Rutherford, the Arapahoe Peyote Roadman, placed his Peyote Chief (a large peyote cactus, with thirteen sections, about three to four inches in diameter) on the altar in front of him. He offered prayers to the Creator and to the fire, after which he began to sing peyote songs. A water drum and peyote rattle were passed around the circle so that others in the group who knew peyote songs could sing more songs. Next a jar of dried powdered peyote was passed around and everyone ingested the acrid-tasting medicine.

Never having ingested peyote before, I simply took a large spoonful and tossed the powdery medicine into my mouth. The acrid-tasting powder coated my mouth, tongue and throat, sticking to the tissue and making it difficult to swallow. Then I observed those who were familiar with this medicine spit into the palm of their hand and roll the powdered substance into small balls. They would toss the balls of peyote towards the back of their mouth, swallowing them without difficulty.

After everyone had ingested the powdered peyote, tea brewed from peyote was passed around the circle. Its effects were very grounding; it made me feel strong, alert and energized. I also felt a deep sense of holiness and cleanliness. Peyote is known to have very positive effects on one's personal behavior and is credited with physical, mental and emotional healing properties. Many people who use peyote report increased personal responsibility and elimination of alcohol and hard drugs in their lives. Research studies done fifty years ago demonstrate peyote to be very effective for treating psychosis, alcohol addiction and various other ailments. Unfortunately, pharmaceutical companies lobbied against further research into peyote and effectively terminated the research.

Throughout the night Rutherford offered prayers for the healing of the boy's eyes as well as for the people of Big Mountain. The rest of us spoke from our hearts as the medicine directed us. We rolled cigarettes made of tobacco wrapped in corn husks for our individual prayers to the fire. Powdered peyote was passed around several times during the night for those who were called by the medicine to ingest more. At midnight my friend, Valerie, the lovely "Water Maiden," entered the teepee, bringing us fresh water to relieve our thirst. She was wearing a white buckskin dress, her shining black hair hanging down over her shoulders. She was radiant and her appearance was uplifting and refreshing. Songs and prayers continued until sunrise, when she returned with bowls of sweet corn mash, venison, and berries to be shared. The meeting continued until mid-morning when we left the teepee for a communal feast.

I was talking with Rutherford just outside the tepee when the young boy came running over excitedly expressing his joy about the great improvement in his eyesight. He thanked Rutherford for the healing he'd received during the night.

No one had touched the boy physically yet somehow, something had effected the workings of his vision. Some would say this was a miraculous healing. Through the effects of the prayers and the medicine, the peyote roadman had facilitated an improvement for the boy that modern medicine had failed to achieve.

Chapter Seventeen

Visions Beyond the Veil

I invited Grandfather Semu to bring his drummers and singers to participate in a conference at Breitenbush that summer. During the week following the conference Grandfather led sacred mushroom ceremonies for a group of us which took place over four consecutive nights at a private residence nearby. Most attendees participated for only one night, but a few of us endured all four nights. Grandfather would always know if anyone planning to participate had any alcohol in their system. One Native man, whom Grandfather had never met, was a heavy drinker. As soon as Grandfather saw him he advised him not to use alcohol for at least a month after the ceremony. I was in regular communication with this man for many years after the ceremony, and he never went back to using alcohol. In fact, he turned his life around, and eventually became a respected leader among his people.

Prior to the ceremony Grandfather said, "When an Indian takes this medicine he immediately goes 'right out,' but for the non-Indian the effect is somewhat different," implying that it affects us differently according to our genetics. We held out our hands and he put enough "medicine" (sacred mushrooms) to fill our palms.

The morning following the fourth night Grandfather spoke to us, saying, "I'm just an old Indian without any formal education, yet you now know there is much more to this world than what we normally see. You have experienced the fourth dimension; the veil was lifted through the medicine. It has a spirit that can reveal what is deep within us, and who we really are." He went on to discuss some of the events of the previous nights as they related to each individual's particular experience. These ceremonies were very powerful and each person's visions were of a personal nature specific to them.

Among the most memorable of my personal visions during those four nights included observing eagles, hawks and other large birds flying around in a huge panorama which opened up before my eyes. Under the influence of the medicine I felt a powerful spiritual presence and knew that the creatures I was witnessing were spiritual entities who existed beyond time and space. What I saw was different each night when the veil was lifted. However, the mood was the same: feelings of awe and connectedness to all life forms. During the fourth night I had a vision of a Mayan temple and witnessed a golden, winged serpent descending the corner stones outside the temple.

While under the effects of the medicine, I had feelings of increased compassion towards other people and other life forms. There was a sense of seeing from a deeper part of myself. Perhaps when the medicine is taken under the proper circumstances it allows us to access another area of our brain, or opens us to a spiritual part of our mind. If that is the case, what we perceive in that state is there all the time, but we are simply unaware of it or it is not accessible to us in normal states of consciousness. If it were, it would be too overwhelming and distracting for us to function and cope with our day-to-day realities. Maybe the veil that is lifted is within our brain, rather than in front of our eyes, as it seemed to me while under the effects of the medicine.

Chapter Eighteen

Manifestations

My second year at Breitenbush, Jennifer, a friend from my childhood whom I hadn't heard from in nearly twenty years, came to visit. We had first met in our early teens at the county fair horse show. We became good friends during our teens, but since we lived thirty miles apart we would only see each other occasionally at horse shows during the summers. Jennifer attended a private school several hours drive from her home so we would correspond by letter throughout the school year. I always looked forward to receiving her letters because of her poetic descriptions and philosophical leanings. Jennifer impressed me as possessing rare qualities of intelligence and curiosity. It seemed like we had a connection or a bond that I had never felt with anyone else. We lost touch with each other in our early twenties when Jennifer married and started a family.

Partly because of my travels and lifestyle, I had lost touch with all the other friends from my younger days. Jennifer was my "oldest" and dearest friend, so our renewed friendship felt reassuring to me, reminding me that some things do endure the test of time. While Jennifer was visiting I introduced her to several Native American friends with whom she made lasting connections. Being very outgoing, she quickly made many other new acquaintances in Oregon, returning from time to time for personal and family vacations.

My three years at Breitenbush had been socially fulfilling, educational, and enjoyable. I deeply enjoyed my time there, meeting many interesting people from varied backgrounds and tribal affiliations and participating in a number of fascinating ceremonies. I made long and lasting relationships. During that time I had two very meaningful relationships with women who visited the retreat center on a regular basis. There were also a few brief romances with young ladies from distant places who were only there for a couple weeks. Again, as at Steamboat Springs, I was completely caught by surprise when a lovely young woman knocked on my door one afternoon. We'd only interacted briefly when she had first arrived two weeks prior. At first I was baffled, but soon it became apparent she was sincere about expressing her tender affections before she left for home. It was of those "we'll never see each other again" kind of thing. I thought, "How very sweet of her." The winter months were somewhat lonelier, since there were fewer visitors to this isolated retreat center.

I was beginning to feel distant and cut off from the rest of the world. The summer and fall seasons were filled with activity, but being isolated there during the long winter months felt stagnating. I had always felt that one should not stay there too long or they would risk a permanent disconnection with society at large. I was ready for a change, wanting to experience more diversity and participate in everyday commonplace realities that were not part of life here in the forest. I moved to Bend in central Oregon and took a very physically demanding job in a lumber-mill.

Jennifer came to visit again that fall and joined Jes, Gaia and me at a peyote ceremony held in central Oregon. As we gathered outside the tepee just before dark, a Native man offered us fresh peyote cactus "buttons". This was the first time I'd eaten fresh peyote. When I bit into one, the acrid juice hit my tongue, and I nearly gagged, but managed to finish chewing it down. It was extremely bitter, and isn't something I would chose to eat out of the context of the ceremony! After the meeting was underway, we ingested dried, powdered peyote, followed by peyote tea.

About midway through the night I saw what appeared to be a white buffalo bull charging towards me through the air. Oddly, what initially impressed me most was its color instead of the phenomena itself. How strange, I thought, that it is white! Then I realized that it was getting close and coming directly at me. I stared, frozen in amazement, fascinated and captivated by the incredible sight of this awesome being galloping rapidly towards me. In what seemed like an instant the bull struck me in the center of my chest with such force that I let out a loud, involuntary UGH! as I was lifted and jolted backwards.

It felt like the spirit buffalo had penetrated my chest. The other participants around me, noticing my jolt and hearing my outcry, asked if I was okay. I told them I was fine, but I was astounded and shaken by what had occurred. In a state of disbelief, I struggled for a moment to explain it away or dismiss it as a creation of my mind. However, the clarity of the vision of the buffalo and especially the physical impact had been too real to dismiss. For the next two nights several of us that had participated in the ceremony had powerful dreams about buffalo.

Soon after that experience I noticed a small advertisement in an issue of "Western Horseman" magazine for a buffalo auction to be held at the Denver Stock Show. Because of the intensity of the buffalo vision and dreams, we began to investigate the possibility of raising buffalo and I made plans to go to the auction.

There were one hundred head of buffalo for sale at the auction and I got to see these massive, wild creatures up close, charging around in the corrals. The experience of being in their presence, sensing the life force emanating from their eyes, their strength, and agility, stimulated my growing interest in these amazing creatures.

I could almost feel their hearts beating within me, their blood running through my veins. It seemed they were connected to something inside my chest cavity. Perhaps the white buffalo bull that had entered me during the peyote ceremony. When I returned to Oregon I was hooked on raising buffalo.

These feelings reminded me of Grandfather's statements regarding "genetic memory". He believed there were something like subconscious memories in our genetic code which are passed down through the generations. There is something about buffalo that is timeless, that perhaps takes us back to another period of history, tens of thousands of years ago when our ancient European ancestors hunted them and undoubtedly had a spiritual connection with them. The beautiful, mystical paintings made over thirty thousand years ago, in caves in southern Europe, are obvious evidence of mankind's long and deep connection to buffalo, also known as bison. Maybe that is why some people are so captivated when they see buffalo. Something deep inside them remembers a connection from the past. For the Native American, that relationship no doubt suffered from the wholesale slaughter of buffalo in the 1800s, nearly wiping them out entirely.

Nevertheless, Native Americans have maintained a deep spiritual connection with the buffalo. Now, with the rapid increase in the population of the herds, that relationship is being presently rekindled.

My friends, Jes and Gaia, also became interested in buffalo, partly due to the effects of the peyote ceremony and also from their subsequent dreams and visions.

For the past several years Jennifer had become personally committed to assisting Indigenous people through a variety of programs: establishing traditional educational opportunities for young people, assisting single mothers with career development, supporting Indigenous art, and sponsoring programs to reduce alcohol and drug abuse.

She also believed buffalo herds could once again become a source for sustainable income and a food supply for certain tribal groups. She wanted to assist in establishing breeding herds of buffalo on Indian reservations. Jennifer felt that establishing a private buffalo herd would allow us to supply buffalo meat and hides for Native American gatherings and ceremonies. Her vision of bringing buffalo back to Indian lands and my calling from the Spirit of the Buffalo were being woven together by some force beyond our individual awareness.

After developing a vague plan to raise buffalo, we began to look for suitable property to establish a herd. We located an abandoned, rundown ranch in central Oregon which had potential, but little else. We felt the ranch could be revitalized to serve a dual purpose: a suitable place for raising buffalo, and as a place for Jennifer's family to vacation. The arrangement was that Jennifer would purchase the property and provide some funding to improve the land so it could be productive. Jes, Gaia, and I would do the hands-on labor to improve the property and manage the herd. Jennifer's participation was a critical aspect in establishing the buffalo ranch.

We moved to the old ranch the spring of 1988 and began to reclaim the property from the tumbleweed. Much time and effort was spent clearing tumbleweed, disking and removing rocks from the fields, planting grass seed and irrigating. We also made improvements and additions to the corrals, repairs to the old ranch house and began fencing pastures. Other necessary projects included getting a well drilled, installing a septic system, replacing the roof on the pump house, repairing the plumbing system and making many improvements to the irrigation system.

Irrigating in the high desert was a constant necessity to establish and maintain pastures. It was also very time consuming with the maintenance of the three large pumps in the pump house, center pivot, several wheel lines, and hundreds of hand-line water pipes. Much of the equipment was in need of repair since it had not been used in years. Needless to say we had our work cut out for us in order to get everything up and running to bring the fields back to life prior to bringing buffalo to the ranch.

On top of these chores, we were completely immersed in learning all we could about buffalo care and management, all the while keeping our focus on raising quality breeding stock. The time and physical requirements consumed us for the next two years. We were building corral facilities, improving pastures, purchasing breeding stock and developing a marketing plan, while still making improvements to the property, and keeping up with the demands of irrigating the fields.

Due to the limited number of buffalo in existence then, and the probable inbreeding that was occurring in isolated herds, one of our goals was to help diversify the bloodlines. People involved in animal husbandry know that animals with similar genetic backgrounds tend to be less resistant to disease and the offspring are less productive. Mixing bloodlines strengthens the offspring and yields more robust stock. To encourage that diversification we planned to purchased good quality breeding stock from ranches in different regions of the country.

Returning to the Denver stock show that winter, I purchased our six buffalo heifers from a ranch in northern Washington State, and a yearling bull from a ranch in eastern Oregon. We continued to bring the old ranch back to life and make the fields lush with grasses for the herd. I traveled to several other ranches in the west to get hands on experience corralling, sorting and breeding stock selection.

Other acquaintances became interested in raising buffalo, but did not have the land or ability to manage the animals. We decided to set up an absentee owner program which functioned as follows: With their monetary investment I purchased buffalo heifers and cows for them and managed the animals. The ranch would keep one half the number of calves born from the absentee owners' cows and the absentee owners would keep the other half.

Through this arrangement we were able to increase the size of our herd without further financial investment on our part and the absentee owner would increase the numbers of their buffalo without paying monthly feeding and management expenses. We located and purchased more buffalo heifers and breeding bulls from ranches in South Dakota and California that were known for having quality breeding stock. At the same time we cleared, fenced, and irrigated more acreage and built more corrals.

It seems there were forces beyond logic and reason at work in initiating this project. Although we developed production and income projections, we were so focused on bringing it all to reality on a physical plane that some of the financial realities eluded us. Further, we hadn't planned for extensive improvements the fields required, all the extra expenses for unexpected repairs, or the realities of supporting ourselves until the operation became financially viable. It takes several years to develop a buffalo breeding program when you start with calves and yearlings, and a couple more years to get production to a level where income exceeds expenses. Our initial verbal agreements were vague and not put down in writing. The lack of clarity regarding our finances left us with different understandings as to how we were to make it work. These misunderstandings eventually created stress and tension for all involved because there were so many uncertainties with respect to cash flow and operating expenses. But our friendships endured these misunderstandings. As

Grandfather Semu once said, "We are here to learn how to get along with one another."

The ranch became a stopover for many Native people traveling to and from conferences and gatherings. Native people learned about things quickly as news spread from camp to camp, and groups of Native people would spend several days at the ranch to rest and have sweat lodge ceremonies. Grandfather Semu said that word had traveled through the Indian camps by the "moccasin telegraph", as he called it. One group of about fifteen people visited for a week as they prepared for a cross-country horse and wagon caravan to Washington D.C. to raise awareness about social and legal injustices toward Indian people.

We would all rise each morning prior to sunrise for prayers and a sacred pipe ceremony before breakfast. Gaia and the other women would prepare meals and care for the children while the men worked on the wagons, cared for the horses and made other preparations. Jes and I continued to focus on the needs of the ranch because there were still a lot of projects we needed to complete. There were times when the impact of our guests became a distraction from things we were trying to accomplish at the ranch. Although I didn't enjoy confrontation, I found it necessary to discuss those issues with the Native people and at times decline their requests.

Some of the Navajo grandmothers, such as Roberta Blackgoat, that came to the ranch were from very isolated areas in Arizona and they didn't speak English. Their children or someone in the group would act as interpreters so we could all communicate. The visitors offered prayers or songs before each meal and some of the elders would pray out loud for twenty minutes or more before we ate. Being very hungry, I'd sometimes grow impatient as the food was getting colder, while these prayers would go on and on, including every species of life known to mankind. At the next meal a younger family member would seemingly try to out-pray their elder. It almost seemed like there was competition to see who could give the longest payers. However, it was very special to me to be in the presence of these elders. They had such a good vibe and we did eventually get to eat.

One afternoon several Native elders sat near the field observing the buffalo herd. One of the grandmothers commented, "As the buffalo are coming back, we are also." It reminded me of my own speech at Mountain Bear's camp.

Chapter Nineteen

Returning to My Roots

Grandfather and Eneke Alish returned to the ranch in the spring of 1991 and stayed there until late fall when they moved back to California for the winter. During that time Grandfather spent his days making several large carvings depicting the Chumash legends of how their people were created through the interaction of one of their gods and the "dolphin people." The Chumash people used to call the dolphins to them and could communicate with them. The Chumash believed they were descended from the dolphins and in the evenings Grandfather would explain the legends and tell stories about his life and the early settlement of California by the Spanish. With Grandfather's permission, Jes recorded many of those evening conversations.

That summer Grandfather led the last and most powerful sacred mushroom ceremony that I had ever participated in. After preparations were completed and I ingested the sacrament many powerful visions came to me during the course of the night, which pertained to my connection to the buffalo. I observed a number of buffalo skulls which seemed to be floating, suspended in the air. They were all very intricately and artistically decorated. Some had inlaid silver or turquoise geometric designs.

As I reveled at the beauty of those "floating" buffalo skulls, I noticed the sensation of warm breath on my right side and heard a deep, steady breathing sound. When I glanced to my right I saw a huge buffalo bull lying next to me with his eyes focused on me. His large head covered with dark shaggy hair was half an arm's length from my chest. The front half of the bull was completely formed and covered with flesh and hair, but from his mid-section on, only his skeletal bones were visible. This was one of the most incredible experiences of my life! I was in complete awe. This was no hallucination. There was a huge, powerful spirit being right next to me exhaling his breath on me. The physical manifestation of this massive, powerful being lying next to me was so sudden and real that it could have been extremely alarming. However, I felt no fear or threat from it; instead there were only feelings of awe, amazement, and a strong connection.

Immediately I knew this was the Spirit of the Buffalo by information that it conveyed to my mind and by its form which was both physical and ethereal. I understood that this was the form and spirit from which all buffalo are born. Its presence was an incredible gift from the Spirit World. The Spirit of the Buffalo was directing what was taking place, I was simply the recipient of its gift of manifestation. This Spirit remained through the night until daybreak before it left me. The veil had been lifted by the medicine and I had seen with spiritual eyes the spirit beings around me. The Buffalo Spirit had blessed me with its presence and its breath. I could feel its presence in my chest and knew it would guide me to do right by these amazing creatures.

Gaia had become deeply involved in Native ways with a group who lived in central Oregon and held weekly sweat lodge ceremonies at the ranch. She also spent months in Arizona taking care of sheep and house sitting for Navaho elders so they could travel to Washington D.C. to try to prevent the removal of Navaho people from their ancestral lands. Jes continued to give time and support to Native ceremonies.

Because we were still building up the herd and there was no income yet from the ranch operation Jes and Gaia eventually found other jobs and moved off the ranch.

By late fall of 1991 everyone else had relocated to other areas and I was now alone on the ranch with forty-five head of buffalo to manage. It was during this time that my dad suffered a serious heart attack back in New York state and I needed to leave the herd to return home. This situation made me aware of the difficulties in leaving the ranch without someone there to keep track of things while I was away.

A few months later Jennifer decided to sell the property. Her children were at an age where they had lost interest in vacationing at the ranch and I was alone and isolated on the ranch, with no one to back me up if I needed to get away. By now I was aware of my aloneness and isolation on the ranch. I needed to make some quick decisions about what to do with the herd. It became apparent that the ranch was a starting point from which we had established a breeding herd; now I felt that it was my calling to raise buffalo in a new locale.

At first I looked for suitable land to lease in central Oregon, but found nothing that was affordable. Having been away from home for fourteen years, only getting back for visits every five years, I felt it was time to move back east. My dad's age and health were factors in that decision, besides missing my siblings and nieces and nephews.

Initially I investigated the possibility of relocating the herd to my brother Bob's farm in northern New York. However, this proved to be too complicated. The animals would need to be blood-tested for tuberculosis and brucellosis, checked for any reactions seventy-two hours later, and shipped across the country within a short time frame. After considering the expense and other complications involved in moving the herd, it made better sense to try to sell the buffalo in Oregon and purchase other buffalo back east. By early summer of 1992, after securing buyers and negotiating sales, I sold the buffalo and reimbursed the absentee owners. In the meantime I arranged for my brother Bob to begin fencing some of his pastures for buffalo I planned to purchase when I returned home.

For two weeks I traveled around Oregon and California visiting friends, before driving back to New York state in mid-July. Upon my arrival home I located another herd of buffalo for sale in the southern part of New York. I spent the rest of the summer fencing Bob's pastures and building corrals, so we would have secure areas to contain the new herd.

After corralling, sorting and loading the buffalo onto trailers we brought them home late in the fall. As the herd increased in numbers I leased two neighboring farms, fenced the pastures and built two more corral systems. With the herd producing forty calves per year, we soon grew the herd to one hundred twenty head.

Two weeks after I arrived home I met Mary Ellen, who was in the area for a short vacation. She relocated here the following spring and we were married eighteen months later. Although she had never worked with livestock before, she became a very willing and capable assistant when we needed to corral, sort, and load buffalo onto trailers.

In the meantime I fenced pastures on land that my ancestors had originally homesteaded in 1803. Five years later we purchased that property along with the old house those ancestors had constructed in the early 1800's. My grandmother had four young children and was pregnant with a fifth child, when my grandfather died suddenly in the early 1920's. The property had been owned and farmed by my family for four generations, but Grandma was not able to keep the farm going after my grandfather passed away, so the property was sold. It felt very special to be raising buffalo on the fields my ancestors had cleared almost two hundred years ago.

Also we now lived in the house where my father and many other relatives had been born.

Although I was confident in the growing interest in the lean, high protein meat buffalo produced, I never expected the increase in demand for buffalo breeding stock to rise as dramatically as it did in the mid-nineties. Prices for young breeding stock shot up quickly, as many cattle ranchers in the West began to switch to raising buffalo.

We sold calves, yearlings and cows to farms and ranches in New York, Pennsylvania, Virginia, West Virginia, Illinois, Connecticut, Vermont, and Saskatchewan, Canada. Demand for buffalo calves was so strong that for a few years we had buyers on waiting lists. We were continuing the original plan to diversify the genetics of our breeding stock, and distribute those bloodlines to various regions of the country. Many other producers were also contributing to this diversification, thus improving the genetic makeup of buffalo herds in the U.S. and Canada and strengthening the future prospects of the species.

It occurred to me that perhaps the buffalo themselves had set the scene for their own comeback. Since few could afford to raise these magnificent, wild beasts without some financial return, there had to be some strong demand for buffalo to motivate ranchers to justify investing in breeding stock and handling facilities. This strong demand was generated by the health consciousness movement in the early nineties, comprised of individuals seeking low fat, high protein red meat.

Cattlemen taking note of this trend, looked to buffalo to supply this new market, and the number of buffalo increased dramatically in both the U.S. and Canada. With the population of buffalo now at levels that would insure their survival, the demand could stabilize, without threat to them. Both the demand for breeding stock, and sale prices dropped off rapidly a couple of years later after the large ranches in the West reached their capacity and began selling off large numbers of animals. My focus had been on raising good-quality breeding stock to distribute to other ranches, but when the market for breeding stock waned, I needed to find other sources of income from the herd. It had not been financial interests that motivated me to raise buffalo and I always remembered those mounted buffalo heads I'd seen as a boy at the Lincoln Memorial in St. Louis. I declined offers to sell buffalo hunts on our land because that didn't fit with my commitment to the herd.

During the late 1990's I developed a local market for our buffalo meat, supplying colleges and universities in the area. This transition carried us through several years while the demand for breeding stock had declined. When the focus became selling meat rather than breeding stock, my interest in raising them solely for butchering waned. I found it increasingly difficult to butcher animals I'd raised as calves and began to reduce the size of the herd by selling brood cows to other local producers.

Not able at first to part with all of the herd, I kept a few of my favorites, and found employment off the farm. Having spent the past twenty plus years fully immersed in raising buffalo I had trouble letting go. But when a local farmer made an offer to purchase the remaining animals and equipment something told me it was the right time to close out the operation. There were several factors involved in that decision, one of them being my age and not wanting Mary Ellen to have to deal with a herd of buffalo if something suddenly happened to me. I felt I had followed that path to its conclusion. It was during this time that the medicine men appeared to me in a vivid dream, stating "We are pleased with what you have done with the buffalo." Then the presence of two medicine men I was very close to began to press upon me to write this memoir, and share their wisdom with whoever might read it.

In retrospect, I suppose one could say the buffalo chose me to raise them, rather than it being my idea. I did help provide them with safe spaces to roam and reproduce, good pasture, feed and clean water. We helped in a small way to increase their numbers, and redistribute their offspring, thus diversifying the genetic pool in other herds and increasing their future prospects for survival.

Charlie, the friend I'd gone west with over thirty years ago was back in town recently. As we briefly reminisced about our journey I reminded him that he never told me the story about the two salesmen who were traveling through the West. He paused for a moment before telling me, "Years ago two salesmen were traveling through the southwest on a bus. As the bus arrived at a general store for a quick rest-stop, the older salesman said to the younger one, 'That old Indian sitting there can remember everything.' 'No one can remember everything,' the younger salesman replied. 'I'll bet you twenty dollars he can,' the older salesman insisted. When they left the general store the senior salesman asked the old Indian sitting on the steps, 'What did you have for breakfast June 17, 1947?' 'Eggs,' answered the old Indian. 'See, I told you he could remember everything,' the senior salesman said. 'Now pay up.' The younger salesman refused, saying, 'Anyone could have said that.' Just then the bus driver ordered everyone back on the bus.

A few years later the young salesman was traveling that route alone. When he arrived at the general store the same old Indian was sitting on the steps. As the salesman walked up the steps he said sarcastically, 'How, Chief!' The old Indian glanced up at him and replied, 'Over easy.'

Finally, as Grandfather Semu liked to say, "Be happy and grow old slowly."

CPSIA information can be obtained
at www.ICGtesting.com
Printed in the USA
LVHW021636110619
620865LV00015B/935

9 780996 394895